HOW TO GET MARRIED

(Without Divorcing your Family)

Also available from HarperCollins for the men:

THE BIG MATCH

Simon Mayo & Martin Wroe

HOW TO GET MARRIED

(Without Divorcing Your Family)

Caron Keating and Janet Ellis

HarperCollins*Publishers*

HarperCollins*Publishers*
77-85 Fulham Palace Road, London W6 8JB

First published in Great Britain
in 1995 by HarperColins*Religious*

1 3 5 7 9 10 8 6 4 2

A catalogue record for this book is
available from the British Library

0551 02773-8

Printed and bound in Great Britain by
Scotprint Limited, Musselburgh, Edinburgh

CONDITIONS OF SALE

Dedication

To our Husbands, Best Men, Best Women
and Assorted Confetti Throwers

Acknowledgements

We would like to thank: Christine Smith, Michelle Worthington, Rev Michael Perry, Rev Jane Austin, John and Russ

Contents

Introduction

Think of this book as the literary equivalent of two paracetamol and a stiff gin. No matter what stage of the proceedings you've reached - whether it's hugging your copy of *Brides* magazine or throttling your mother-in-law - take heart, help is at hand. Born out of our own experiences and endless cups of tea, we aim to help you pick your way through the minefield of the marriage maze.

Whether you're planning the society event of the decade or a quick pint at the Ferret and Firkin, your wedding is a very important day. But remember, it's just a starting point - the really important bit is what happens next. Styles of wedding may come and go, but marriage is always in fashion.

Though far from perfect - after all a lot of married life is about coping with the extremely anti-social habits of your loved one, and their refusal to admit you are the finest person that ever lived - we still reckon it's a Good Thing. But a big dress, a romantic honeymoon, and a fully-fitted kitchen are not good enough reasons to start sending out invitations. Far be it from us to pontificate on the state of wedlock, but suffice it to say that it's not to be entered into lightly. That said, once you've decided to spend the rest of your life with someone, for all the right reasons, then you owe it to yourself to have the best possible day - you may have a few quid, you may have an open cheque-book (preferably someone else's), it doesn't matter.

With three of our own weddings and a sea of taffeta between us, we feel somewhat qualified to offer our suggestions for the traditional and not so traditional wedding. There are a few hard and fast rules to getting hitched but after that, you're on your own. Except, that is, for your intended, your friends, your families ... and us, of course.

Let's state at this early stage that this book is girls' talk. Of course, it takes two to marry, but unless things change radically, it's us girls who really get Down to Business where weddings are concerned. Show him appropriate chapters, by all means; read bits aloud together if it suits you; but we'll be surprised if the boys get all irate at not having a book like this written especially for them. We suggested it to our chaps, but we haven't a printable reply ... yet.

If at the end of this you manage to get married happily, remain on good terms with your nearest and dearest, and open your wedding album with a smile on your face, we'll have done our job.

WARNING!

THIS COULD BE A BIG MISTAKE

Are You Sure You're Doing the Right Thing?

Before we go any further, and for those of you for whom it is not too late - are you *quite* sure you want to get married?

Is this the person you want to share your PMT with? Are you making this public statement just because you want a new frock and are fed up fending off enquiries on the subject of when is he going to make an honest woman of you? - nice as that sort of chat can be.

If your idea of a good night out is dancing round your handbag, slightly tipsy on Babycham, before snogging the local talent, then perhaps you're not quite ready to settle down. Might you not be happier squeezing yourself into designer goodies during your lunch hour, rather than spending your time reading *Marvellous Meals with Mince*?

Are you sure you want someone who owns an Aston Villa bobble hat to be the father of your children? Yes? - then read on.

TERMS OF ENGAGEMENT

Natural Selection

If you have yet to select a partner, we're not sure that we can be of much help. If you haven't got anyone specific in mind, chucking a bit of old apple peel over your shoulder seems to be as good a method of selection as any. Whichever initial it forms when it lands will undoubtedly lead you straight to Mr Right. But don't blame us if it doesn't spell out Prince Edward, no matter how many times you throw it.

In fact, the contents of your kitchen cupboards are likely to lead you to true love faster than our Cilla and all her blind dates. Peas, unfortunately not the frozen kind, are unlikely diviners of your marital fate, according to legend. Should you happen to be shelling peas and chance upon a pod containing nine perfect specimens, pop it by the front door and take careful note of which man comes in next - it's your husband-to-be. Equally unglamorous, but probably just as reliable, is that well-known traditional practice of scratching your boyfriend's initials on a few onions and seeing which sprouts first. This is particularly suitable for those with lots of boyfriends, onions and spare time.

Marriage is a wonderful invention; but there again so is a bicycle repair kit.

Billy Connolly

Personally we recommend, for pure novelty value, the wishbone approach. Drill a small hole through the flat part that joins the legs of the bone. Perch it on the bridge of your nose and then try to thread the hole as if you were threading a needle. The number of unsuccessful attempts you make equals the number of years before you will get married - and makes you cross-eyed in the process!

But don't think that the men get away lightly. Apparently, a man should prick the skin of an orange all over and put it in his armpit overnight. The next day he should give the orange to a girl he desires without telling her where it has been or why he's offering it. If she eats the fruit, she will return his love (either that or her taste-buds are seriously defective).

We did consult Mrs Beeton, the oracle on all matters of the heart and domesticity, who was able to offer these sound words of advice:

Let neither rank nor fortune, not the finest order of intellect, nor yet the most winning manners induce you to accept the addresses of an irreligious man ... also do not marry a weak man; he seldom listens to the voice of reason and most painful it must be to a woman to have to blush for her husband and feel uneasy every time he opens his lips.

Don't say we never told you ...

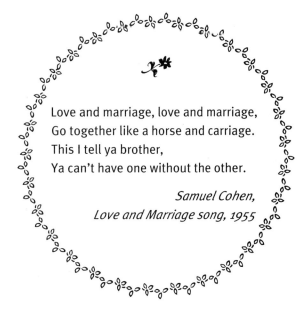

Love and marriage, love and marriage,
Go together like a horse and carriage.
This I tell ya brother,
Ya can't have one without the other.

*Samuel Cohen,
Love and Marriage song, 1955*

Barbara Cartland, a woman who was forced to spend much of her early life fending off her fifty proposals of marriage, believes that the reason men don't propose with quite the eagerness they used to is because these days they think, 'Why buy a cow when you can milk it?' She is also convinced that all women long to be carried away into the desert by a sheikh. So just as you were thinking that marriages were made in heaven, you discover that it really happens in some stinking sand-pit, with a man who, deep down, prefers his camel.

But it could be worse. For centuries love was seen as an emotional indulgence and had very little to do with marriage. The bride was nothing more than a bit of property to be captured, exchanged or bought and shackled to the man whom her parents or tribe thought most suitable - in other words the one with the most dosh. In Anglo-Saxon times the prospective husband paid his bride's father, not to buy her but to compensate the father for the loss of his daughter's services. 'Love' was nothing more than an emotional sideline indulged in with extra-marital partners: sometimes frowned upon, more often encouraged.

These days we cling to the quaint idea that 'lurve' should come into marriage somewhere. Teen mags and song lyrics would have us believe that every passing male could be The One. Just remember to look the length of the counter before you make your final selection. Of course you can always take the direct approach and phone up someone you've had your eye on.

Marriages Made In ... Jail

There are certain members of your family, no matter how fond of them you've become, where marrying them is not a good idea - particularly as it's against the law. Originally this was introduced to help prevent family defects being passed on, although if appearances are anything to go by, many families seem to have got round this problem. But now the law has changed to include other relationships, between people not connected by blood but still bound by emotional ties. You will not thank your mother if she suddenly absconds with the boy you've adored since the Lower Sixth. Equally, your grandmother will take a dim view of your attempts to drag your grandfather up the aisle. In these cases it is preferable that the law gets you, before your family's wrath boils over.

Most are fairly obvious, but if you're in the slightest doubt, check it out. People you can't marry include:

father
mother
brother
sister
father's father's wife
mother's father's wife
wife's father's mother
wife's son's daughter
mother's mother
daughter's son's wife
daughter's daughter's husband

People we wouldn't advise you to marry, if you want it to last:

Zsa Zsa Gabor
Any of the Queen's children

The other criteria, which may be harder to

fulfil, is that you're both sound of mind (luckily no-one's devised a test), both over sixteen, and neither of you is married to anyone else.

Once you've found your partner, don't be surprised if you start to see them in a different light - something akin to a 160 megawatt spotlight. This is entirely normal - after all, everyone else is busy scrutinizing your relationship and your future, so it's hardly surprising if you start to do the same. Even if you've known each other for years it's somehow different realizing that you're going to be lumbered with his not-so-appealing habits for life. Everybody feels a bit apprehensive about the commitment involved, but unless you have serious doubts just breathe deeply and hope the moment will pass.

So, after all those hours of not-so-subtle hinting, bursting into tears when your friends got married, and your father holding a small shotgun to his head, he has finally sunk to his knees and uttered those immortal words, 'My darling Celia, you are the sun, the moon, the stars. You are everything that is important, all that it is beautiful. Without you I am nothing etc., etc.' At least, that's what he means to say. It may emerge as, 'D'ya fancy get hitched or what?'

It's surprising what a profound effect such a simple enquiry can have. Assuming that the answer is 'yes', and you've now made the transition from girlfriend to fiancée. How long you remain in this engaged state is up to you.

You're Engaged

The average length of an engagement is seven months. There are of course those who don't like to rush things. The longest-ever

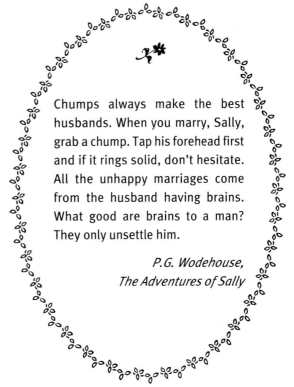

Chumps always make the best husbands. When you marry, Sally, grab a chump. Tap his forehead first and if it rings solid, don't hesitate. All the unhappy marriages come from the husband having brains. What good are brains to a man? They only unsettle him.

P.G. Wodehouse,
The Adventures of Sally

engagement was Octavio Guillen and Adriana Martinez. They married in Mexico City after a sixty-seven-year engagement - they were both eighty-two! Opinions vary greatly and will be influenced by numerous factors, like your boyfriend's ability to debate the merits of Saint and Greavsie with the male members of your family (a big plus); or his reputation as the most engaged man in town - in which case your mother may suggest a bit of a breathing space, like twenty years.

These days an engagement often comes as quite a surprise so it is unlikely that your father's permission has been granted to give your hand, or indeed any other bit of your body, to your intended. Of course in the good old days, along with your hand came a suitable dowry. This could range from a couple of pigs to a sizeable chunk of England. There are still those who come complete with a small mansion in the country, but today it's more likely to be a Magimix and a chipped Tufty Club mug.

In some cultures the dowry is the girl's weight in silver and gold coins, which presumably encourages the sort of diet Demis Roussous would be hard pushed to get through in the lead up to the wedding. A Bolivian tin millionaire elevated himself to Father of the Decade status in 1992 when he paid a dowry of £8 million for his daughter Elena. It was either a very generous gesture or Elena made Moby Dick look like a tadpole. Either way it entitled him to work his way through their drinks cabinet and show his running medals any time.

If you're hoping that your father will pay for the wedding, it's probably a good idea to warn him well in advance, so that he can investigate second mortgages and reconcile himself to making do with his old golf clubs for another twenty years. Breaking the news over a large drink usually helps to soften the blow. If you're under eighteen, by law you have to get your folks' permission.

Amongst the less legalistic rules affecting the engaged are that they should not be photographed together, the bride-to-be should not sign with her married name, nor should she knit a sweater for her fiancé. The latter especially is known to lead to engagement disaster.

An engagement really puts everyone in the mood for your wedding - you included. Of course this is the time when you sort things out legally, financially and frivolously. It also adds excitement to the time you spend with your fiancée - so try to make sure you're not totally concerned with lists and obligations. To be serious for a minute, you are facing the future together - concentrate on the things you're looking forward to and talk about the things that worry you. You may never have had an opportunity before to talk seriously about children, money, relationships and your dreams for the future. Once you're married it may be too late to discover that your ideals are poles apart.

We're not suggesting that you marry a mirror image of yourself - you may be surprised how receptive to new ideas you are - but there's a big difference between being receptive and being blind. If there are things about your man you're planning to change -

> Mr Mybug, however, did ask Rennet to marry him. He said that, by God, D.H. Lawrence was right when he had said there must be a dumb, dull, bitter belly-tension between a man and a woman, and how else could this be achieved save in the long monotony of marriage.
>
> *Sheila Gibbons,*
> *Cold Comfort Farm*

forget it, divorce courts are full of people who had similar ideas.

Choosing the Ring

If you're anything like us, no sooner have you muttered 'Yes, all right', than you'll be checking there's enough petrol in the car to get you to the local jewellers. Fortunately, engagement rings date back to Roman times, and cannot be dismissed by your fiancé's bank manager as a passing fancy.

You may already have an intimate knowledge of his bank balance. If not, try and get some idea of what he's prepared to spend rather than having your first argument about money (there'll be many more), in front of an interested bunch of shop assistants.

Having had it drummed into us over the years that diamonds really are a 'girl's best friend', and 'for ever', most of us don't look much further when choosing a ring. However, this particular love token only became popular in the ninteenth century, not so much for its romantic associations and promise of true love, but because imported South African stones were cheap. Trust a man to spot that ... nothing changes.

If you're going for meaning rather than value, you quaint old-fashioned thing, the following list might help:

Birthstones and their meaning

Month	Stone	Meaning
January	Garnet	Constancy
February	Amethyst	Sincerity
March	Bloodstone	Courage
April	Diamond	Lasting love
May	Emerald	Hope, success
June	Pearl	Health
July	Ruby	Love
August	Sardonyx	Married happiness
September	Sapphire	Wisdom
October	Opal	Hope
November	Topaz	Faithfulness
December	Turquoise	Harmony

The Victorians were keen to illustrate their love in a more graphic way and actually spelt out messages in their stones.

Love Me: Lapiz Lazuli, Opal, Verdantique, Emerald, Moonstone, Epidote

Regard: Ruby, Emerald, Garnet, Amethyst, Ruby, Diamond

Dearest: Diamond, Emerald, Amethyst, Ruby, Emerald, Sapphire, Tourmaline

For reasons of sentiment or shortage of cash, your husband-to-be may produce the family heirloom ring which his mother had always hinted he could use, in the days when marriage seemed a remote possibility. If you're lucky, this will turn out to be a beautiful antique, but if you really don't like it - and it takes a brave girl to say so - a tactful chat pointing out that a ring you choose together might have more sentimental value, could get you over this hurdle.

Antique rings are also another possibility, and because many people are superstitious about the risk of inheriting someone else's fortunes, you can pick up a bargain. This particularly applies to wedding rings.

If your tastes run to the more exotic - twisted barbed wire, ruby-encrusted ring pulls, that sort of thing - and you're prepared to pay a bit extra, you could always have your ring made. The jeweller might also do a deal with a matching wedding ring.

Our forefathers believed that a vein in the fourth finger of the left hand ran straight to the heart and so wedding rings have always been worn on that finger. Advances in medicinal science may not have found this to be correct but it takes more than a few old scientists to shift such a strong belief.

In these callous modern times, one school of thought would have us believe that a ring is a sign of male ownership rather than love. You can draw your own conclusions. Suffice it to say that wild horses or crowbars would not part us from our rings. If owning jewellery given by chaps is a problem to you, we'd be delighted to help out - our addresses are at the back of the book.

We don't want to put a dampener on the situation, but it's as well to know that having got this object of beauty wedged firmly on your finger, the return of the ring breaks the contract. We recommend, however, the Zsa Zsa Gabor approach: 'Darlink, I've never hated any man enough to give the ring back.'

In-Laws - Not Outlaws

Unless you marry a self-contained orphan, you'll very soon realize that your fiancé comes attached to people whom you will quickly learn to call your in-laws. Now, take a deep breath.

In an ideal world, you will feel part of his family, with a lovely new mother and father, maybe a darling granny and a squad of good-looking, muscular brothers-in-law-to-be (some hope). Initially they might even make a welcome change from your own. However, the reality often is that all those endearing little habits, which you found so funny prior to the wedding, become as amusing as Tony Blackburn's jokes. Even the sweetest prospective mother-in-law may reveal sides to her character over the engagement period that qualify her less for a 'Nanette Newman Niceness Award' than a place in the chamber of horrors. After all, Les Dawson must have got his jokes from somewhere.

Remember, the thought of somebody else lovingly sorting through her son's old socks, and telling him to stop picking his nose, may make her feel emotional. So intense is the rivalry between some women and their future daughter-in-laws that in some African cultures the mother-in-law is stuck in a hut far away from the family home when she comes to visit! If you can manage to see her side of things and unclench your teeth long enough to throw a smile in her direction from time to time, life will be so much more pleasant.

It's also worth bearing in mind that your views on the wedding are unlikely to coincide with hers. It's bad enough that you are attempting to wrench the light of her life from her loving grasp; just don't think she doesn't know that once married he'll waste away to nothing, you'll forget his daily Halib Orange, and don't know how he likes his gravy (or anything for that matter). This is no reflection on your character. There are in existence mothers-in-law who would regard Mother Teresa as a shameless gold-digger. Just stick to your guns and don't be put off. However, a little tact and minor compromises can go a long way towards smoothing ruffled feathers.

FAMOUS MOTHERS-IN-LAW

'No make-up ... Coke-bottle glasses ... brown hair in no apparent style' was how Virginia Kelley dismissed her daughter-in-law Hillary Clinton. Hillary was equally unimpressed: 'Here was a woman who got up at 4.30 every morning to put on her false eyelashes,' she recalls. 'I couldn't imagine what we would have in common.'

When Sylvester Stallone brought home his intended in the awesome shape of Brigitte Nielsen, his mother Jackie announced to the world: 'I didn't raise my son to marry someone like that. I don't like her and I've begged Sly to dump her.'

Raquel Welch saved her breath and, in a triumph of upstaging, managed to grab all the limelight when she arrived late at her son's wedding just managing to wear a low-cut little black dress.

FATHERS-IN-LAW

If you do feel the icy wind of maternal disapproval roaring round your ankles the minute you step into the family seat, the best place to take shelter is behind your prospective father-in-law. For us girls, fathers-in-law are a piece of cake.

You can become the daughter he never had (assuming that he doesn't have any of course), and remind him of his youth. He will play you his favourite Val Doonican records and give you cuttings from the garden, all in recognition of the very great favour you are doing him, i.e. removing once and for all the millstone which has been hanging round his neck for the last twenty-four years! - the person who 'borrowed' and wrecked his car, never cut his grass, drank his last can of lager,

and threw up all over his newly painted bedroom. Oh yes - he'll let you have his son with pleasure.

PARENTS MEETING

While you and your beloved may have a lot in common this doesn't mean that your respective parents will get on like a house on fire. This is nothing new: Shakespeare spotted it years ago. While the tragedy of Romeo and Juliet would not have been averted if Mr and Mrs Montague and the Capulets had got together over a drop of Harveys Bristol Cream, there's a lot to be said for an informal social gathering, even if the only outcome is that the mothers-in-law agree not to wear the same colour on the big day. At least they'll be able to recognize each other at the wedding and not be reduced to enquiring loudly who the woman under the odd-looking hat is.

Although they'd rather crawl over broken glass than admit to it, sadly this is where a strongly competitive element may creep into the proceedings and is likely to manifest itself in the worst possible way from your point of view. We are referring to the showing of the baby photos. And it doesn't stop there, of course. Next will come the ballet certificates, first teeth, appendix stitches, cycling proficiency badge, cub woggle etc., etc. Oh yes, they'll all be there; on display like some freak side-show. The point of this shameless exhibition of (usually) motherly pride is to let the other party know that their son/daughter are extremely fortunate to be marrying this umblemished specimen of humanity. Of course, in an ideal world they would have been getting hitched to royalty. But there again, the traffic around Buckingham Palace has always been a bit of a problem; and what if the children inherit those ears?; quite apart from the fact that the Queen's children first marriages to fail is 100 per cent.

In other words, no one is ever good enough for any mother's child.

The value of marriage is not that adults produce children but that children produce adults.

Peter De Vries

Spreading the News

There are lots of ways to spread the glad tidings, presuming there's anyone left to tell once your mother's finished. An announcement in the paper, whether it's *The Times* or *Farmers Weekly*, saves a fortune on phone calls and ends all that speculation about it ever happening. If you want to be proper about it, the correct wording is:

Mr H. Ford and Miss J.M. Ellis
The engagement is announced between
Harrison Ford,
son of Mr and Mrs Wilbur Ford
of Alabama
and
Miss Janet Michelle,
daughter of Mr and Mrs Mike Ellis
of The Maltings, Middlesnendon, Bucks.

This gets the message across in terms that the Palace would approve of. When the parents on either side are divorced or if one of them has died, it is usual to make this clear in the wording: 'son of Mr Wilbur Ford of Alabama and Mrs Ethel Ford of Texas' or 'son of Mr Wilbur Ford and the late Mrs Ethel Ford'.

But if the formal approach isn't really your style, you won't get a visit from the etiquette police if you simply put:

Harrison Ford and Janet Ellis are delighted to annouce their engagement...

(At least Janet looks thrilled, we're not so sure about Harrison.)

Alternative announcements range from bribing the local DJ, leaflets tossed from a hot air balloon, printed T-shirts and a large tattoo, to advertising hoardings, a town crier, or a small plane trailing a banner. You could even write a few letters. In the rush to tell your friends, don't leave it to your parents to break the news to Grandma or Great-Aunt Gertie. Some consideration now will also ease the way and come in handy for when you want to announce later on that you're opting for a bungy-jump wedding.

In bygone years the girl's delighted parents hosted an engagement party to celebrate the glad tidings. This is a custom which seems to have fallen from favour in recent years. As an interesting experiment in watching a grown man cry, try asking your father to revive it.

IDEAL PLANS, REALISTIC COSTS

Setting the Date

First things first. There's nothing like setting a date to make an engagement finite - in other words, the vague 'when we get married' begins to fade away as the countdown clock starts to tick.

In the olden days weddings mostly took place on weekdays or Bank Holidays as the working class were not entitled to a holiday. This meant that the most popular days for getting married were Christmas Day, Boxing day or Easter Sunday and Monday. Easter had the added bonus of bringing with it great tax advantages. It's encouraging to know that the age of romance has always been alive and well!

Today most people set the wedding date according to the first Saturday when the church, venue and all important members of the wedding party are free. However, one particular tradition takes a different approach suggesting a day when all the planets are positioned to indicate a happy and prosperous future. Each day of the week is associated with a different planet.

Saturday: Saturn's day

Saturn's influence is heavy and serious, with much hard work and responsibility, but also with much material award.

Sunday: Sun's day

A good day as the marriage would take all the bright, warm radiance of the sun into itself.

Monday: Moon's day

The moon's day benefits the wife more than the husband.

Tuesday: Mars' day

Tuesday would make for a very active, go-getting marriage, although probably with plenty of arguments.

Wednesday: Mercury's day

Mercury's day would be good for children, but it could involve an element of change-ability. Some people might prefer something steadier and more constant.

Thursday: Jupiter's day

Thursday would make for wealth, but might also mean having to travel and, maybe, live far away from home.

Friday: Venus' day

The most romantic day to marry as Venus is the goddess of love. In Norway, where tradition has obviously not forgotten the planets, Friday is the most popular day for weddings.

It doesn't really matter which day you decide to get married on because there's bound to be some aged relative who will shake their head, convinced that you're condemning yourselves to a life of gloom and doom - particularly if you opt for a Saturday. An old rhyme referring to the lucky days for the ceremony is as follows:

> Monday for health
> Tuesday for wealth
> Wednesday, the best day of all;
> Thursday for losses
> Friday for crosses
> Saturday, no luck at all!

As Saturday is precisely the day most of the population goes for, it could well explain the divorce rate.

Once you've cursed your relationship for ever by deciding on a Saturday, you can ladle even more doom about yourselves by selecting the wrong month. If you're a real

It is thought that the best time of the month to marry is when the moon is waxing and preferably before its first quarter, i.e. within the week following a new moon. This information is easily obtained as most diaries and calendars show the phases of the moon with little symbols.

glutton for punishment how about May? Said to be a time when 'whores and knaves go to church and every ass is in love'. In Roman times it was the month for extra-marital nookie (we can think of a few objectionable people who'd like this custom revived). In fact, the most cheerful words on the subject are: 'Marry in May, rue for aye.'

Towards the end of the year the outlook isn't quite so bleak:

> Marry in September's shine,
>   your living will be rich and fine;
> If in October you do marry,
>   love will come but riches tarry;
> If you wed in bleak November,
>   only joy will you remember;
> When December's showers fall fast,
>   marry and true love will last.

Strangely enough, the months when the majority of people get married - June, July and August - have been completely left out. Draw from this what conclusions you will.

There are also many traditional beliefs surrounding the time of day that a couple choose to get married. Most important occasions such as enthronements, openings of Parliament, etc., take place at around eleven o'clock, the time of day when the sun is reaching its highest point in the sky and is therefore at its most powerful. A wedding solemnized at this time is said to ensure that the couple will go on to enjoy happiness and success together.

To hold a ceremony later in the day suggests that the sun is closer to setting and therefore less powerful. Others believe that a wedding held around three o'clock in the afternoon is felt to mean that married life will involve big changes for both partners, but also that the union will be more passionate than weddings held earlier. Weddings held just before sunset make a strong personal bond for the couple concerned but less of an impact in the public eye.

Family birthdays and anniversaries are favourite dates for weddings and there are, of course, those superstitious types who'll let the tea leaves decide when they should tie the knot. But in reality the impatient bride-to-be, or her mother, will eventually tell everyone to stop being so stupid and superstitious and she will decide the date and arrange the whole thing. No wonder so many weddings coincide with the FA Cup Final and the British Open.

What Type of Wedding?

It might sound obvious to talk about the sort of wedding you want, but remember, it's *your* day and it's important you feel as happy about it as possible. Don't be pushed into having someone else's dream wedding. Without wishing to cast aspersions, the word 'mother' springs to mind. Also worth bearing in mind are the feelings of one other fairly important person - the groom.

If you've always dreamt of a service in St Paul's complete with an angelic choir of seven-year-olds, but your fiancé shudders at the thought of meeting more than an audience of two - sort it out early. Any Jeremy Beadle fans amongst you (there must be one somewhere) will doubtless have laughed themselves stupid at the sight of grooms keeling over from nerves, sickness or fright. This is a strange phenomena which seems to affect only the male of the species and only in wedding situations. Put him in a football crowd of 5,000 beery fans or in front of twelve visiting darts teams - no problem. But ask him to stand in front of a friendly throng of friends and relatives, next to the woman he loves, and he swoons like some Victorian heroine. There's no easy cure. If telling him to pull himself together doesn't work, Valium may be the only answer ... for you!

Also in line for the Valium treatment could be your mother. Ever since your conception, it's likely that she'll have been plotting the big white number with you centre stage looking like a huge meringue. It will be very difficult for her to come to terms with the fact that not only have you set your heart on a red sheath dress but that Las Vegas is where you plan to plight your troth. Skilful negotiation may be the answer, but with Uncle Gerard's gambling history, the red sheath in St Mark's, Ickenham, may be a far cheaper and peaceable option.

BEACH WEDDINGS

Various aspects of the traditional church or registry office wedding are considered in the next chapter. However the idea of getting married with your feet planted in the sand, surrounded by swaying palms and a steel band playing gently, accompanied by the sound of waves caressing the beach, is extremely tempting. No arguments, no going-away outfit, no cans tied to the back of your car, no speeches and crying mothers; just the perfectly blissful day you'd always dreamt of with the two of you entwined in a tropical paradise.

This kind of wedding works best for Richard Branson types who come complete with their own island, or for very rich orphans who don't have to put up with their mothers thumbing wistfully through their wedding albums.

The first few couples who braved the wrath of their families probably had a wonderful time, but these days it's more of a hit-and-miss affair. Tour operators always keen to make a quick buck, have hijacked the idea and turned romance in the sun into two glasses of cheap champagne, a wilting garland and the cry of 'next please'. They tend to schedule these ceremonies for exactly the moment when your sunburn is at its most painful, your hair is limp and lifeless from salt water, and the lobster hue of your face clashes horribly with the dazzling white of your carefully packed dress. As the suntan oil dries on the marriage certificate and the champagne-produced headache starts to make you a bit weepy, you may even regret that the rest of your family aren't there. Suddenly the thought of Aunt Maude paddling in the surf isn't so terrible.

If you're still determined - you'll need three things: factor 47 suncream, very understanding families, and a long time to go through the brochures. Anyway, think of the money you'll save on a separate honeymoon.

Locations guaranteed to tempt even the most dedicated choir member include:

St Lucia	Mombasa
Seychelles	Mauritius
Orlando	Jamaica
Barbados	Domincan Republic
Antigua	Grenada
St Kitts	Cancun, Mexico
Thailand	

The cost of the actual wedding varies, depending on which hotel you're staying at, but it's likely to be upwards of £350 per couple on top of the actual holiday price. Check that the supplementary charge includes the following:

- all administration, documentation and handling arrangements made in the UK and your destination
- ceremony, marriage licence, certificate and all registrar fees
- best man, on request (could be a huge advantage, this one!)
- something sparkling to toast the bride and groom
- wedding cake
- flowers
- location, decoration
- possible video of ceremony, photographs
- celebration dinner

Obviously there may be some additional extras which can be sorted out and paid for locally, ranging from live music to additional catering and ... who knows?

To get married abroad you have to have been staying at the resort for a minimum of six working days before the necessary licence can be issued. As these weddings are a fairly recent phenomenon, there's no set etiquette as to how to spend your six pre-wedding days ... Anyway, it'll take that long for the creases to fall out of your dress. Think in terms of staying for about a fortnight.

Apart from your sunblock and Diacalm, for the actual ceremony, you'll need:

- passports - the first six pages of both passports (or the last six if a new EC passport)
- both birth certificates; if you've changed your name by deed poll, proof is required
- proof of the absolute, if one party is a divorcee.
- a death certificate in the case of widow/widower
- evidence of parental consent, if under the age of 18 - in the form of a statutory declaration stamped and signed by a solicitor
- both Christian/other names and surnames and respective professions or occupations

SOMETHING A BIT DIFFERENT

If, on the other hand, it's tack and a brush with stardom that you're after, then how about Las Vegas? One of the few places where you can get married and divorced again all in the same day.

Other types of exotic or unusual weddings include under water, in a hot air balloon, on a ski slope, free-falling parachuting, on horse back, during the London marathon, at sea, at Stonehenge, or even in a car showroom.

A change in the law in April 1995 will mean that there will be more choice of places to get married in venues that think they meet the licencing requirements - decorous and sensible! Such venues will be able to apply for a license and a registrar will then officiate just as they do in a registry office.

Places that have been hosting receptions will doubtless consider extending their services and the most popular will be booked up miles in advance. If there's somewhere special you like that isn't licensed, you'll have to ask them to apply. It doesn't quite mean that you can get married in your living room like they do in American films - but watch this space!

But no matter where or how you tie the knot, just make sure the event has some meaning or significance for the two of you, otherwise you might regret it later. The bottom line is, it's your day and while you want everyone to enjoy themselves, you're never going to please everybody. Hopefully they'll be so happy for you that the three weeks you spent barely on speaking terms will be forgotten. This is how it *should* work, at least in theory.

Counting the Cost

At one time weddings were a very bad time, financially, for the parents of the bride, unless of course they were the Duke and Duchess of Westminster. News of an engagement was met with a sharp intake of breath and a feeble 'Congratulations' before hurriedly checking out the possibility of a second mortgage. This may be the time when your father starts mentioning Gretna Green on regular occasions and suggests that elopement is probably a very good idea. When questioned he will confess that, oddly enough, this dates back to your fifth birthday party - when the boy next door showed rather too much interest in playing doctors and nurses and your dad realized there was a potential bride lurking beneath those pigtails.

If your parents have always seemed very old-fashioned in every aspect of life, now is the time when they could well shock you with their strikingly modern attitudes. In other words, your father has no intention of paying for the lot. Apparently though, there are some fathers still in existence who insist on paying for the whole thing. If you spring from one of these you have our blessing and deep envy.

As there seems to be a trend these days for people to get married when they're older, richer and more experienced, more and more couples are paying for, if not the entire proceedings, then at least a good chunk of it. It's quite likely that when your husband carries you over the threshold, it's the one that you've been stepping across completely unaided for many months, if not years. Therefore, it seems a little illogical to expect your parents to cough up for the whole thing, particularly if it's not the first time you've ventured up the aisle, and the novelty may have worn off as far as your parents are concerned. (In cases of extreme repetition, you may have problems persuading them to come at all.) Anyway, if everyone pays what they can, all should feel equally involved emotionally and financially.

Although it's boring to discuss money, before you get carried away and start planning a week-long street party, here comes the bad news: membership to the Aisle High Club doesn't come cheap. The average cost of a wedding these days is £12,000. Some weddings cost ten times as much as that - a recent wedding in London worked out at £250,000 for 300 guests! You may think you've calculated right down to the last petal of confetti, but there's always something else: another bottle of asprin, another hat or two for your mother.

Your father won't thank us for this, but traditionally he pays for:

- your clothes
- your car
- the reception
- the cake
- the flowers
- the photos and video
- Alka Seltzer
- a garter
- the bridesmaid's dresses
- wedding stationery
- numerous boxes of Kleenex
- and, oh yes, those extra hats

The bridegroom, who gets away fairly lightly at this stage but will have to pay through the nose whenever he has a daughter of his own, forks out for:

- the church
- his clothes
- his car
- the ring
- the buttonholes
- presents for the bridesmaids and best man
- and the honeymoon ... bad luck guys!

The fortunate bride only has to buy her husband's ring.

Naturally it is impossible to predict exactly the cost of an average wedding. We're all from different financial backgrounds and consequently everyone's maximum budget varies enormously. However, the following table is based on a wedding held at a village church in the Midlands, with a reception for a hundred guests in a three-star hotel:

Local newspaper announcement	18.00
Stationery	198.00
Postage	15.00
Bride's clothes	995.00
Bride's hair and make-up	35.00
Groom's clothes (hired)	86.00
Bridesmaid (x 1)	150.00
Going-away outfit	400.00
Car hire (x 2)	246.00
Flowers	375.50
Church fees	92.00
Rings	200.00
Presents for attendants	50.00
Photographer, prints, album	1,012.68
Video	245.00
Reception (x 100) including food, drink, staff, evening buffet	4,385.00
Cake	155.30
Favours	110.00
Disco/band	150.00
Wedding insurance	52.00
Total	£8,970.48

You don't need to leave the country or even your neighbourbood to arrange a wedding that everyone, including you, will look back on fondly. But we'd be the last to pretend that money doesn't make a difference. Should you arrange a wedding for less than a fiver and then win the National Lottery, you may well decide to pop a bit more into the coffers. But there is a lot to be said for cutting your coat to fit the cloth. In other words, have a really good divorce ... After all, a wedding is the start of your married life together, not the beginning of a joint overdraft nor even a huge farewell party for your single life.

Ten Ways to cut the cost (and stay happy)

1 Hire, borrow or buy a dress second-hand. If it must be new, look for something plain. Beading and frills add to the cost and you can always add your own. You could also investigate clothing auctions.

2 Ask an artistic friend or an impoverished art student to design the invitations and have them printed up yourself.

3 Go direct to the flower market rather than the local florist for the flowers. It means an early start, but much cheaper flowers. Ask talented friends to supply greenery and help arrange them, or the church where you are getting married, is bound to have an army of flower ladies who'll be delighted to step in at a fraction of the cost of a professional.

4 If the bridesmaids' mothers offer to pay for their dresses - let them. They can always wear them to parties afterwards. You'll probably never get around to adapting yours for other events but the average six-year-old has no such qualms and will probably have to be persuaded out of rather than into the dress for the foreseeable future. Including bedtime.

5 Leave disposable cameras on each table at the reception, instead of extending the photographer's booking, and ask friends to send you copies of their best shots.

6 Book one car rather than a fleet and appoint a car monitor to make sure everybody gets transport. (You can always bribe them to leave certain relatives stranded). Or why not revive an old tradition and walk to the church? We have it on good authority that the gathering of well-wishers as you pass by really gets the proceedings off to a great start. Obviously this is only suitable for those within bouquet-throwing distance of the church and possessing reasonably flat shoes ... Stiletto wearers need not apply.

7 The reception doesn't need to be a huge, sit-down, silver service affair. People

have come to celebrate your marriage, which they can do as well over a plate of sandwiches in the garden as smoked salmon in a five-star hotel. If it's a summer wedding, why not suggest everyone brings a picnic; or if you want a strictly indoor affair and china plates, why not book a restaurant? Arrange a menu and inform your guests in advance of the cost. Alternatively, have a small reception for family and close friends followed by a large bring-a-bottle party for everyone else.

8 Search your family tree for any vaguely Greek connections and revive that marvellous old custom of pinning money to the bride's dress. With any luck you'll be one of the few brides to make a few bob on your wedding day.

9 Answer small ads for TV shows looking for wedding couples - *The Big Breakfast* and *Challenge Anneka* are always good for this - but be prepared to stage a few rows to keep them happy, and to have a cameraman attached to the hem of your dress.

10 Sell your pictures to *Hello* magazine (see Jane Seymour for details!).

For radical cost-cutting - elope.

SACRED AND LEGAL

Today we all have different opinions on where we want our wedding to take place, but many people feel the desire to get married in church, not only because of their religious beliefs and the spiritual significance, but also because they see their marriage as an extremely important event in their lives and want to give it the very best start and most solid foundations possible. This they feel they can achieve with a church service.

Chatting to the Cloth

You and your fiance may not be from the same religious denomination, so this might need to be accommodated and sorted out well in advance. It is worth noting that the minister of the church in which you are marrying will expect to take the service.

Therefore if your groom is, for example, a Roman Catholic and wishes his priest to be present or give a sermon, please be sure to discuss this with your minister and ask him/her to extend the invitation to your groom's priest. (The chances are that if you are marrying a man from another denomination, the families - even in this modern day and age - will prefer a male minister to marry you.)

For those of you whose last brush with religion was playing half a donkey in the Nativity play, it's time to re-acquaint yourself with the gentlemen (or women) in the black dress (or frayed jeans, if they're a 'happy clappy'). Worrying thoughts tend to cross the average couple's minds when they approach the minister, like: Will he/she mind that we're not regular churchgoers? Does it matter that we wouldn't do well in a religious knowledge test? Perhaps we can't get married here after all!

There are two extreme types of clergy: firstly, those who treat the whole thing so desperately seriously that they almost succeed in converting you to celibacy for life. These types are trained to spot someone in search of a pretty backdrop from a great distance. They will expect to see you in church every week, participating in the Bring-and-Buy sale and coffee mornings; they will quiz you on the New Testament and administer four-hour one-way chats on the meaning of marriage. They are perfectly entitled to do this. After all, it's a small price to pay in return for a good photo album. If that is your main motive - it serves you right.

The other type, who undoubtedly hang out in less sought-after surroundings, are an altogether more lenient shower, secure in the knowledge that you must be coming to them for religious reasons or because your mother thought it was a good idea. The only thing they ask is that you turn up on the day and that your cheque for the organ player doesn't bounce. In other words, they're not at all that interested in you. Avoid these types if at all possible. You want someone who will want to get to know you and who will want to make the service as full of meaning and significance for you as they can.

Most vicars will be only too happy to put your mind at rest, and if you're doing it for the right reasons will be pleased to guide you through. If you do come up against an awkward vicar, there are ways round it. It's worth approaching your parish council rather than giving up.

Religion and the Law

Each church is independent and although the bishop of the diocese sets out the policy for those within it, the minister of each church is in charge of his/her domain. However there are certain restrictions that cannot be avoided, even by the most open-minded minister, as they are matters of law decreed by Parliament.

It is possible to apply for a Special Licence in some circumstances, but be warned; this is not available to couples who want to marry in a specific church just because it happens to be good for photos! Also, the law states that if one half of the couple has been married before they cannot marry by Special Licence, they must have Banns (the publication or the public announcement of the engaged couple's intention to marry) called.

The cloth stress the importance of an ordered existence, and would like us all to listen to the still, small voice of calm. This can be a good antidote to the frenetic efforts you will be making to get your reception, photographer, bridesmaids dresses, wedding list and invitations organized

The first question the still small voice will be asking is what age you are. The minimum legal age for getting married is sixteen years, although you will need the written consent of your parents or guardian, if you are under eighteen. The marriage must take place in a registered place of worship (church, synagogue, etc.), or district registery office, using an authorized religious or civil ceremony. The ceremony must take place in front of two witnesses over the age of eighteen.

Marriages can take place between 8 a.m. and 6 p.m., at the discretion of the person performing the ceremony. Registry Offices are closed on Sundays. Exceptions to these rules in England and Wales include marriages by Special Licence, and Jewish and Quaker weddings.

In Scotland there is much more freedom of choice. It is possible to get married in any church in Scotland, regardless of where you live, and parental consent is not required if you are between the ages of sixteen and eighteen. Whether you are having a religious or a civil wedding, you must apply (in person or in writing) for a marriage schedule by giving notice to the local Registrar of where you want to marry, at least fifteen days (but no longer than three weeks) beforehand. Banns

are no longer legally required in Scotland, and the contents of the Church of Scotland ceremony and where it is to be held are entirely at the discretion of the minister. He/she may marry you at home or in a hotel, and is unlikely to refuse second-time-around marriages.

All denominations have their own requirements so it is essential to see your minister as soon as possible to ascertain what these are. Most Christian ceremonies are similar, with maybe slight changes in vows to distinguish between them. For all, apart from Anglican weddings, you must obtain a certificate or certificate of licence from the local Superintendant Registrar. In some cases, if the person performing the marriage isn't authorized to register it, the Registrar may have to be present.

THE CHURCH OF ENGLAND

Provided that one of the couple is baptized and either lives in the parish or is on the electoral roll, they may marry in that parish church. The minimum notice is six weeks. The minister will arrange that the Banns are read out on three consecutive Sundays. The ceremony must take place within three months of the Banns being called.

If you wish to get married in a church which is not in either partner's parish, you will have to apply to be put on the electoral roll or take up residence in the parish for the period over which Banns are read. Or you can apply for an ecclesiastical licence from your local diocesan council, which means that you can dispense with the formality of having the Banns called at all.

Banns are the sole legal necessity for Church of England weddings since this is the only religion where the minister acts both as Registrar of State (on behalf of the State) and as priest of the church (acting on behalf of the church).

THE ROMAN CATHOLIC CHURCH

See your priest at least two to three months before you plan to marry, in order to received adequate instruction. Don't forget to take along baptism and confirmation certificates. If only one partner is Catholic, permission to marry in a non-Catholic church may be given, but is entirely at the discretion of the priest. The same applies to someone who is not a Catholic but wishes to marry in a Catholic church. It is sometimes possible for ministers of other denominations to be involved in a Catholic ceremony.

NON-CONFORMIST OR FREE CHURCHES

Banns are not necessary in these churches, and you may get married in any church which is the place of worship for either you or your partner, whether you live in the parish or not. An outside Registrar may have to be present.

ORTHODOX CHURCHES

These churches include Serbian, Greek, Russian, Romanian, Bulgarian and Cypriot, and their ceremonies are rich in tradition and ritual. It is best to take advice on their specific requirements directly from the local church authorities.

THE QUAKERS

The Religious Society of Friends keep their ceremonies as simple as possible, in fact they have hardly changed since the seventeenth century. The wedding is held at a worship meeting in which the couple make a declaration of marrigae. No minister or priest conducts the service. If either partner is not a member of the Society, their application must be approved in writing by two adult members of the Society.

These are both religious and civil ceremonies and therefore two applications for marriage are necessary. When applying to the religious authority under which the ceremony is taking place, the couple must be accompanied by at least one witness (preferably a parent) and have the relevant documents (birth certificates, parent's Jewish marriage lines, etc.) with them. Most ceremonies take place in a synagogue but can be performed anywhere, so long as they are under a *chuppah*.

Second Marriages

Widows and widowers may remarry in a church or synagogue. However, it is often difficult for many people who have been married and divorced to come to terms with the fact that they may not be able to remarry in church. Unfortunately, while legally divorced people are at liberty to marry again, the law of the Church of England does not generally permit this, believing that the vows originally given to each other are for life. But, ultimately it is the decision of your minister and the Bishop.

Some vicars are happy to carry out second marriages so long as there was evidence of a clear break between relationships before remarriage. After all, the majority of single people approaching a minister with regards to planning their wedding have had relationships before, and in many circumstances they have lived with other partners prior to finding their bride or groom. Clearly all ministers have differing views on how a marriage service should be conducted and who they will marry, but if you don't ask, you'll never know.

Whilst some clergy are willing to remarry divorced people in certain circumstances, others are not. Some, however, are willing to offer a Service of Blessing after a civil marriage. (Although the Catholic Church does not provide this, an Anglican minister may agree to hold such a service if one or both partners are Catholic.) This can follow on directly from a registry office ceremony or be arranged for a later date. The service usually includes prayers, a blessing and a gospel reading, and as such caters for the spiritual side of the marriage.

The Church has had to adjust over the years to meet the changing patterns of relationships. It is more concerned with helping people to rebuild their lives constructively than passing judgement. Often partners come to second marriages feeling even more committed and determined to succeed in their new relationship. It is with this in mind that the majority of churches run a marriage preparation course for would-be brides and grooms.

These sessions offer practical, down-to-earth advice on a myriad of issues including money, conflict, God, love and sex. They provide a good opportunity, amid all the foaming and frothing over wedding lists, dress-fittings, placating of relatives, etc. to take time out for getting to know each other in a bit more depth. You'll be surprised at what's on offer in marriage preparation classes, and in our mind, they're another Good Thing.

You wouldn't sit a GCSE exam without at least going to some of the classes, yet it is quite astonishing how many couples sail into marriage on a cloud of tulle and fond hopes, not having any real clue about the commitment they are making. Most couples, at the end of the sessions, still know that they want to get married as planned, but for some it is an eye-opener to the fact that perhaps they are not ready to make a lifetime's commitment quite yet - if at all!

Doing Your Own Thing

So you've met the minister and he/she likes you and you like him/her. Most importantly, you've decided that the spiritual significance of a church service is you and your man's idea of the best start to married life. Perhaps at this point it is useful to dispel a few misapprehensions about church weddings.

People often associate the term 'church wedding' with great expense, lots of rules and regulations, a huge frothy white dress and a lavish reception. These are just optional extras which have grown up over the years and now often surround a marriage ceremony in church. If you do not wish or cannot financially stretch to all these trappings there is no reason why you and your chap can't still get married in a church in your best clothes and celebrate with friends and family afterwards over a simple meal or even a pint and sandwich down at your local.

However, when you consider that the cheapest professional photographer alone could set you back about £300, then getting the whole church service for around £264 including organist, bells, choir and flowers suddenly seems like very good value indeed - and that's if you're only looking at the commercial side of your big day. Indeed the cost can be reduced even further as you don't necessarily have to have an organist, choir and bells. Also, if hardship is the one factor preventing a couple from getting married in church, the minister is at liberty to waive the fees.

So having got rid of the argument that a

church wedding is too expensive, the next thing that worries many people about a traditional church wedding may be that it will be too rigid and stuffy for their liking. Most clergy are only too aware that you might feel like this. Try talking to your minister to see if you can 'design' your wedding service to suit you.

Some sections will be negotiable, the most obvious example being the bit about promising to obey. Others have to stay, like the confirmation by bride and groom of their will to marry each other, the exchange of vows or promises, the giving and receiving of a ring or rings, and the joining of hands with each other by the minister. As these are the best bits anyway, we would question the sanity of any couple wishing to drop them.

You can choose either the new or the old service, the main difference being that there is more equality in the new service-men and women come together on equal terms in the eyes of God. The old service put its emphasis on marriage being for children first, then companionship, and finally love. In the days of high infant mortality, this was an understandable ordering of priorities. The new service is not only much simpler but puts the love element of marriage first, followed by companionship and finally children.

Once the couple have made their vows to each other, they give and receive a ring or rings. The wedding ring is viewed as a symbol of unending love, and in the church service the giving and receiving is done in the form of a prayer ending with the words 'within the love of God, Father, Son and Holy Spirit'. However many changes are made to the wedding service, this is one bit that will remain intact.

These days there is also an opportunity for the bride to give a ring to her groom, whereas this was not an option previously. The new emphasis on love, equality and intimacy can also be seen by the fact that the bride and groom now face each other during the service instead of the minister.

At this point you might think we're stating the obvious, but it is important to the Church and in terms of the law that both partners understand what is being said to them during the civil or religious service and that they know what they are committing to (then there can be no excuses later!). It is for this reason that if you or your partner are foreign or do not have a great command of the English language, you should discuss a bilingual service with your minster. Likewise, if either of you are deaf and you or the minster cannot 'sign', you will be given the legal requirements of the service to read and then you can respond accordingly.

Once you have decided with your minster which version of the marriage service to have, he/she will explain the vows and go through the ceremony with you. When looking at the alternatives and options available to you - for example, music, poems and readings - bear in mind that they should be suitable for the event. In that way there should be little problem in having them accepted for your wedding service.

MUSIC

Deciding what sort of music to have at the wedding is one of the acid tests of your relationship. The song that makes you misty-eyed can have the same effect on him as a cup of cold sick. So while you're arguing the toss between Donny Osmond crooning 'Puppy Love' and some well-loved Anthrax ditty urging mothers to let out their daughters, remember - there's the whole church service to sort out.

The sort of music you choose very much sets the tone for the whole day, but it may be limited by the ability of the organist and the attitude of your vicar. While some might not object to you including highlights from Rodgers and Hammerstein, figuring that love is love whether it's directed towards God or Doris Day, others may feel that *Hymns Ancient and Modern* covers every eventuality.

Probably the best way to incorporate a favourite song is to make it a solo turn - the entire congregation warbling 'True Love' can end up sounding like a bad night down at the karaoke club.

There's a lot to be said for familiar hymns - you know, the ones you last sang at school assembly, which is almost certainly the last time half your guests will have heard them. Of course some are more suitable than others - 'Fight the Good Fight' isn't exactly the sentiment to aim for. Others to steer towards include:

Love Divine, All loves Excelling
Morning has Broken
O Perfect Love
All Things Bright and Beautiful
Come Down, O Love Divine
I Vow to Thee My Country
Praise my Soul the King of Heaven
The Lord is my Shepherd
Immortal, Invisible
For the Beauty of the Earth
Jesus Shall Reign
Lead Us, Heavenly Father, Lead Us

If you don't know many hymns or have any favourites, grill your family. Your granny's bound to have one she loves.

You'll need a tune to walk up the aisle to, another for when you're leaving, and something to entertain everyone while you're signing the register. This could be a singing friend, relation, dog or the choir; failing that, the organist's Grade Eight examination piece.

With the entrance music, it's difficult to beat a bit of tradition. All those tried and tested tunes allow you to walk in a dignified way without falling over your train and will last until you reach the altar. More importantly, they signify your arrival and put an end to all the chatting and waving. They also drown out the sobs of assorted relatives and heartbroken exes.

Here are a few suggestions to get you started:

Before the service

Elgar	'Nimrod' from the *Enigma Variations*
Purcell	Prelude in G
Bach	Jesu Joy of Man's Desiring
Handel	Water Music

The Entrance of the Bride

Handel	Arrival of the Queen of Sheba
Mozart	'Wedding March' from *The Marriage of Figaro*
Parry	Bridal March
Purcell	Fanfare
Clarke	Trumpet Voluntary
Wagner	'Bridal March' from *Lohengrin*

Having got yourself and your nearest and dearest into the church and through the service, the law is now very keen to get something in writing. You'll need some music to keep the congregation entertained while you both sign the register and you struggle to remember the spelling of your new surname. There are no hard and fast rules here as to what you showcase, although Uncle Gerald's rendition of 'Your Cheating Heart' may not be appropriate at this moment. Traditional pieces include:

Handel	'Air' from *Water Music*
Schubert	Ave Maria
Gershwin	'Summertime' from *Porgy and Bess*
Handel	Minuet (Berenice)

Suggestions for music to accompany the Recessional could include any of the above plus anything else that takes your fancy, bearing in mind that if it could suit the occasion, so much the better. If you sing in a choir, play in a rock band or have a favourite aunt who sings Motown, you could enlist their services and ask them to perform. Just check with the vicar: you wouldn't want Led Zeppelin's greatest hits to shatter stained glass windows.

INVOLVING OTHERS IN THE SERVICE

With discussion beforehand there are many ways of involving those special to you in the service. Decide whether or not you want to be given away or whether you would prefer to walk down the aisle with your groom. If you do want to be given away, then who's going to do it? Obviously for many there is no question about it - this is Dad's big moment, but many brides don't have a father. Be sure to choose someone who's really special to you, and don't assume that they have to be male - many mums or best friends would love to be by your side.

Lots of couples already have children when they get married. Speak to your minister about how they can be involved in the service. Perhaps they can walk down the

---

The bridesmaids are representatives of the 'guards' who once accompanied the bridal parties in case they should be attacked by enemies wanting to carry off the bride. It is said that the bridesmaid who catches the bridal bouquet can look forward to being married herself within a year, but if any of these attendants should stumble on the way to the altar, unfortunately the saying, 'Always the bridesmaid never the bride' will apply to them. A matron of honour is said to bring particular luck to a bride as she symbolizes the happy state of matrimony.

Myths, superstitions and old customs have survived remarkably intact throughout the centuries, although today's bride may not know that blue was deemed a lucky colour or that confetti symbolizes fertility. Paper confetti and rose petals are a modern substitute for rice and corn, the symbol of a full harvest and therefore abundance.

aisle with you and your groom and be a completely integral part of the proceedings. Janet's eleven-month-old son Jack was the best man, with the ring in his romper suit ... he carried out his duties superbly, but left the speech-making to others.

Also worth consideration is the exiting from the church. Everyone in the wedding party should be partnered as they leave the church. This should be given some thought as possibly a parent may have died or parents are divorced and not on good terms. Contrary to what you may have read in a bridal magazine, there are no set rules as to who should escort who out of church. If the traditional partnering is likely to cause problems, then abandon it all together and create partnerships that work for you and your families.

ANY LOOSE ENDS?

It is at this point that fees and a rehearsal should be discussed with your minister, as well as his/her views on photography, video, confetti, etc. Many ministers are now happy for the wedding service to be photographed or filmed on video for posterity. If this is the case in your church, before any filming can take place you must obtain a special licence for copyright purposes by telephoning Christian Copyright Licensing, (01323) 417711, or faxing them (01323) 417722. For a more detailed look at photographers and videos, see chapter 6.

Even if your intention is for nothing more than a picturesque setting, it would be nice if you and the priest at least recognize each other. You'll probably feel much better if you know your way around the church and can find the aisle and altar without too much difficulty.

Most clergy organize a brief rehearsal just before the big day to reduce the chances of the groom and best man marrying each other by mistake, and to avoid an unseemly scrum around the altar. Experience shows that most people spend this time in a state of tears, blind panic or hysterical laughter. Better to get it all out beforehand, and with any luck, some of what you're told will sink in.

The Boring Bit: Legal Matters

A REGISTRY OFFICE WEDDING

The fastest route to marriage for those in a hurry, due to reasons they might rather keep to themselves, is a registry office. If in a moment of wild abandon, or drunkeness, you accept the invitation from Mr Percival in Accounts to be 'his, his and his alone', it is possible to get married in a matter of days from the moment his knee touched the carpet. We can only hope that you have given the prospect of marriage all due care and con-sideration, and can only suggest that if not, you look out for the yet-to-be published sequel to this book, tentatively entitled *Divorce: The Best Bits*.

There's a whole host of reasons why people choose to get married in a registry office, ranging from the purely financial to complicated timetables or extended families. While the idea of spontaneously dashing into the Chelsea Town Hall on the Kings Road,

grabbing a couple of witnesses on the way, sounds romantic, even this type of wedding takes a bit of planning.

You can either marry by Certificate or by Licence. To marry by Licence you need to have lived in the district for at least seven days before applying. If residence is in seperate districts, applications to each district is necessary. You can then marry after twenty-one clear days of giving notice. If, however, marriage is by Certificate with Licence, one of the couple must have lived for fifteen days in the area and the partner must be in the country when the notice is given. You can then dispense with the twenty-one days wait. Both types of Certifi-cate are valid for three months and in each case the marriage must take place in the district where the notice was given.

It takes two to make a marriage a success and only one a failure.

Lord Samuel

You can't book any earlier than three months beforehand, but do it as soon as you can - particularly if you want to get married between May and September.

The office is open between 8 a.m. and 6 p.m., although those opting for the 8 a.m. time slot really will be testing the loyalty of their friends, not to mention their own constitution when it comes to toasting the happy couple. The ceremony is short, approximately fifteen minutes, and the couple must have two adult witnesses. It is also advisable to check beforehand as to how many guests you may invite.

THE MARRIAGE CONTRACT

You may think it very unromantic to have a marriage contract, or that there are some people who can't quite bear the idea of their beloved getting their mitts on their dosh. Nevertheless, it is a good idea to have a little 'chat' about who's going to pay for what and whether or not you're going to have a joint bank account, that sort of thing.

Money is one of the most contraversial subjects in any relationship, closely followed in marriage by how often you phone and/or visit your mother, and whether or not he can display his Under-Twelves Pea Shooting trophy. It is best to have the discussion now, while you're still gazing into each other's eyes and feel fairly generous towards each other. Indeed, while you still *like* each other. So get the money talk over with, and we don't think you need to go on to work out who does the hoovering, or collects the Chinese takeaway, or sews on buttons, or remembers loo paper. Cynically, you know the answer to most of these questions anyway, and if you decide all that now, what are you going to talk about for the rest of your lives?

It is common to hear people talk about the wedding ceremony as 'tying the knot'. This derives from an actual description of what used to happen in a Babylonian wedding. Here a thread was taken from the bride's dress and another from the groom's clothes and these were tied together to symbolize their union.

CHANGING YOUR NAME

Most girls assume that marriage inevitably means losing something. We mean your maiden name, of course. But it's not a legal requirement, just a matter of choice. Of course if you've spent your life saddled with a dreadful name, you'll probably be only too glad to get shot of it. Indeed, this may be the main reason for your getting hitched in the first place. Just be prepared to go through all those forms, from passports and the electoral roll to re-registering with your doctor and your bank.

These days an increasing number of women are opting to keep their maiden names, particularly in the workplace, and become Mrs Whatever for joint domestic matters like carpets and children. Be prepared for a hitherto unmined seam of die-hard conservatism in the ranks of both families. Some will either feel you're rejecting a perfectly good surname or not accepting the entire marriage deal.

At the end of the day, it's whatever you and your husband feel happiest with. To find out how we feel about it, have a look at the front cover of the book.

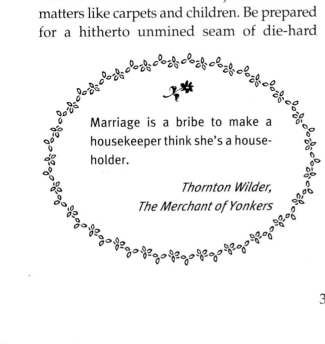

Marriage is a bribe to make a housekeeper think she's a householder.

Thornton Wilder,
The Merchant of Yonkers

PUTTING ON THE RITZ

Once the actual wedding ceremony has been discussed and decided upon you can turn your thoughts to the celebration of your new marital state. In other words, the wedding bash. Whether you're planning a quiet little affair for just family and close friends or a massive event at a country house hotel, you'll still need to consider many of the same things, like who to invite, what sort of food and drink to offer your guests, and whether music and speeches will feature at all.

The Guest List

Brace yourself: this is where you will need to summon up every ounce of tact and diplomacy. In principle, it sounds easy to draw up a list of your closest friends and favourite aunties. You may even foolishly believe that you and your chap are the ones doing the inviting. Be under no illusion - you are not.

There are a few people whom you really ought to invite, like your parents. After that, there are several options:

- an intimate gathering for 2,000 of your dearest pals
- just the family (somebody must think this is a good idea)
- just friends (there have been no known survivors from this one)
- edited highlights from amongst your family and friends
- two tickets to Gretna Green if the going gets really tough

In reality, if the bride's parents are forking out for the whole affair, don't be fazed by the sight of half the Rotary Club, as you glide up the aisle. Just console yourself with the thought of all those extra flan dishes. Even worse are those relatives you never knew existed, or hoped they didn't - the ones who claim they last saw you in nappies and insist on sharing the experience with your friends. There will undoubtedly be the same assortment on HIS side, and because it's unlikely that you know them, they'll seem even worse.

Compromise is the only answer. Let both sides draw up a list and you may as well draw names out of a hat because there's always going to be someone you've forgotten or haven't got room for. They will never, ever forgive you, no matter how many crumbled bits of cake you send them afterwards. There are some situations that not even a UN peace-keeping force would tackle.

If you've decided to do without holidays for the next ten years to pay for the entire thing yourselves, you might imagine that this entitles you to a bigger say in the guest list. What you have to remember is that wedding guests are an ungrateful lot who have no regard for whose hard-earned cash is paying for their chicken vol-au-vents and wine. But look at it from your their point of view: it'll be difficult for uninvited relatives to keep smiling when the subject of your wedding comes up at family gatherings for the next twenty years. For the sake of family politics it's probably worth listening to your mother,

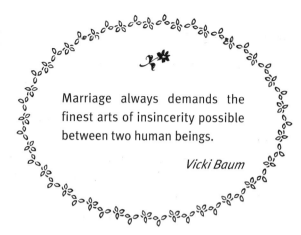

Marriage always demands the finest arts of insincerity possible between two human beings.

Vicki Baum

who will know from bitter experience that you leave Cousin Beryl off the list at your peril.

CHILDREN

The other potential minefield is whether to invite children or to adopt a Herod-like attitude to their presence. Those who own a few will take a dim view of their absence and may remind you that one of the original purposes for the state of matrimony was procreation. On the other hand, some people's children make Bart Simpson look like a choirboy, and will not enhance any part of the day.

Ex-boyfriends

Your partner may take umbrage at your intention to invite all your exes, no matter that they are now your good friends. The sound of broken-hearted men sobbing throughout your wedding vows would lend a tragic air to the proceedings. Even worse would be the mocking laughter or mutterings of 'rather him than me'. Much better that they are left to their own devices outside the church.

Divorced Parents

If your parents are divorced, this is when you'll discover if they've buried the hatchet or have been regularly sharpening it. Despite the happy event you're all celebrating, if there is friction between your estranged parents it could spoil the day. There's nothing worse than standing at the altar, pledging eternal love to the sound of your family growling at each other behind you. Just because their own marrigae was a disaster, it doesn't give anyone license to get yours off to a bad start.

It's worthwhile talking it out well in advance and encouraging a few puffs of a peace pipe, even if the effects have worn off by the reception and the bubbly has taken over. Try pointing out that it's supposed to be a happy day, and for everyone's comfort and safety their co-operation is appreciated. However acrimonious it all may seem, in most cases they manage to get on well enough on the big day to avoid actual assault.

We can't give you any guidelines about inviting new partners or children. Unfortunately it's up to you to try and sort out some kind of amicable solution well in advance. There are no hard and fast rules about this and it really does depend on individual circumstances. While in an ideal world it would be terrific if everybody 'played ball', life is not like *The Waltons* and there will always be someone who refuses to co-operate as a matter of principle.

If your parents are not on speaking terms, you may have to reconcile yourself to one party being absent .... Worse, if your family at large won't come to an agreement about a cessation of hostilities on one flippin' day of the year, then as much as you may want them to be there, you may have to accept that it's simply not possible. It's their loss.

The Venue

It doesn't matter what time of day you get married, the 'do' afterwards is always referred to as the wedding breakfast. The choice of venue is initially dictated by money, numbers and your own taste, in that order. Apart from that, the options are endless.

A BAKER'S DOZEN OF PLACES TO HAVE A RECEPTION

1   A marquee in your back garden
2   The town hall
3   Museums
4   The Dorchester, or local equivalent
5   The room above your local
6   The church hall (cheap and within walking distance usually)
7   The beach
8   Top deck of a bus
9   The nursery slopes in Les Arcs ski resort
10   The Guinness brewery (guarantees maximum attendance and no danger of running out)
11   Ice rink
12   Scout hut
13   Bowling alley

Marquee: works best in good weather. Once you've decided on the price you can make the reception as lavish or as simple as you want, funds allowing. Plus points include the fact that with canvas walls you can easily squeeze in a few extra people, and there'll be no–one calling last orders. More about marquees later.

Town Hall: very often, these have wonderful function rooms concealed within, and are well set to cater for large numbers of people. Maybe the Mayor will lend the luxury limo for the day, (maybe not). As they are regarded as something of public amenity, the cost should be reasonable.

Museums: these days, museums are much more clued up, commercially, than they once were, and if you inquire about the possibility of hiring them now they may produce a glossy brochure. Even those which are more off-the-beaten-track are keen to encourage events out of hours. In London, for example, museums as diverse as the Natural History Museum (hours of fun to be had comparing older relatives to dinosaurs) or the London Dungeon are available. If you're looking for a really unusual venue, how about Britain's oldest operating theatre? Your food will taste even better served from an ancient operating table. For all these museums, the prices vary enormously, but it's always worth asking.

Top deck of a bus: best suited to very small receptions .... Standing room only might be bearable on the way home, but isn't the ideal way to relax your guests. Plus points include great views and no gate crashers.

Other moving locations worth considering:

River boats - although you're stuck with everyone for the duration.

Hot air balloons - perfect for friend-free couples

Steam trains - free anorak and notebook provided

Aeroplane - obviously you need vast wealth and an exciting destination. It's no good partying madly in the sky only to land in Luton. Most likely contender: Richard Branson and his island - though interested parties take note, he's already spoken for.

Sublime locations: if there's a building or a beauty spot that you've always loved, be bold and find out if you can use it. Very often there'll be a guarded 'yes', and maybe a few restrictions. For example, there's nothing to stop you having a picnic in a royal park, but no choruses of 'Here Comes the Bride' are allowed as an ancient by-law forbids music.

There must have been a first time for all the more exotic venues, so do see if you can use the one you fancy. One of the nicest weddings we went to was in a wonderful Victorian conservatory in a botanical gardens. You can find one on the outskirts of most cities.

For those with illusions of grandeur, investigate your local National Trust castle. Such dwellings tend to come complete with beautiful gardens and imposing rooms large enough to seat big parties - grand enough to impress even your most cynical relatives.

HOTELS

If you're committed to a Saturday wedding you may find that the hotel you've set your heart on is the one every bride in the country has pictured herself floating around and has a five-year waiting list. This is either the excuse you've been looking for as a breathing space, or a crashing disappointment. You have two options: you could move your wedding to a week day, and face the wrath of the gainfully employed (this also serves the useful purpose of keeping attendance figures down); or you could find somewhere else.

Hotels are a very popular choice as they come complete with car parks, caterers, loos, paper hankies, enough chairs, and people trained to avert their eyes from the more extreme behaviour shown by your guests and to clear up afterwards. In their eagerness to cater for the most disorganized and unimaginative wedding parties, some hotels will provide the cake, a room to change, and a dustbin lid to tie on the back of the car. In extreme cases they will even write the best man's speech and, should you be left in the lurch, lay on a groom.

The other advantage, particularly to the hotel, is that they provide ideal accommodation for your out-of-town guests. So, when overcome by the emotion of the occasion, your guests can fall upstairs. Sometimes they do this in pairs - not necessarily the ones they arrived in, a practice which can result in more weddings. If you've decided to 'go away' to a relative-free zone, make sure you appoint a gossip gatherer to fill you in on all the gory details of what happened after you left.

The down side is the cost. Unless money is no object, you may have to juggle the numbers and menus, and be reduced to discussing the merits of wild smoked salmon as opposed to the presence of your old head girl. Although undoubtedly it will not be the first menu they show you, they will have a cheaper version. It's surprising how elastic the guest : vol-au-vent ratio can be. This also applies to the drink. In an ideal world nothing but Bollinger would flow; in real life, one glass per person to toast the now poverty-stricken family surrounded by something sparkling, possibly mineral water is closer to the mark.

If you haven't got a favourite hotel, the best thing to do is ask around and visit places you like the look of. Compare atmosphere, prices, menus and facilities, like whether they've got a plug for your karaoke machine. Don't forget to discuss numbers - it's no good settling on a lovely, intimate room if there isn't enough space for the big band, let alone for you to throw the bouquet. It's better to have more space than not enough.

To ensure a relationship with the hotel which lasts longer than the reception:

1 Check well in advance for added costs like VAT and services. Ascertain when final payment is required.

2 Establish whether they'll be taking a Cinderella approach and turfing everyone out at an appointed hour. This needs to be especially clear if there's another wedding party lining up outside and the staff are forced to begin hoovering throughout the speeches.

Hall or home

If what you call home happens to be the type of place the rest of us expect to pay an admission charge to enter, you probably won't look further than the ballroom or the garden as a venue for your reception. Even if you don't live in a baronial hall, so long as you've got enough chairs, plates and loos, and can cope with the numbers and feeding them, a reception at home can be very intimate. The other advantage is that you can spend as much or as little as you like.

If you figure you'll have too many guests to squeeze into your house, of if you just like the idea of celebrating under canvas, a marquee is what you want. This is not recommended for those with a handkerchief-sized plot. Marquees weren't designed to be a snug fit, nor to be erected on the side of Ben Nevis - you need a large smooth area, preferably close to the house. Also, to bear in mind is the availability of loos. And what happens if it rains? - will your guests find themselves anchored by their stilettos as your lawn turns to mud? Likewise, the marquee itself will need a floor and possibly heaters.

Oh and lights! It wasn't until lunchtime on a friend's wedding day that she realized no one had organized any lights for the marquee. The prospect of the guests staggering round in pitch black, groping around to find their partners, wasn't an appealing one, although in hindsight it might have been rather fun. Anyway, after a small panic we managed to find a local shop that lent us some.

There are a variety of styles and sizes, ranging from very big to enormous, so if yours is a relatively small reception, don't force everybody to play 'hunt the guest' under yards of tarpaulin. They also come with different coloured linings, so if you are trying to colour co-ordinate the day, you can have a marquee to match. As with everything else, shop around and negotiate the best price, remembering to include tables, chairs, flooring and delivery, and erection and dismantling charges. Don't forget to make a firm booking early on, especially during the summer months.

If your home is part of a housing estate rather than a stately home you should spare a thought for your neighbours (a *kindly* thought, we might add). You may not want to run the guantlet of frosty glares and wagging tongues for ever more, so figure on a little consideration along the way. Politely informing your near neighbours of the possiblity of more noise and frivolity than usual just may stay their hands as they reach for the phone to ring the police. Better yet, invite a few along and get them on your side. And don't forget to work out car parking arrangements. Your life may be in danger if the best man decides to leave his old banger on your neighbour's prize petunias.

RESTAURANTS

If you're reading this whilst hanging from the ninth floor of a tower block or in a mounting state of panic, there is at least one more option. A favourite restaurant could well be the ideal place. Depending on how many guests are coming, you can either take over the whole place or corner off an area. They'll probably be happy to work out a menu for you and might even negotiate some sort of deal for the drink. And the problem of transport shouldn't be a problem if the restaurant is near to car parks or public transport.

Basically, if you've got enough money, you can hold a reception anywhere - within reason. Your mother may not be able to see the attraction of the scout hut or the bus depot where you met, but don't feel you have to be restricted by convention. A venue which isn't used to hosting receptions may take a lot of work and time, but if your hearts are set on it and you feel it will really make your day special, then it's worth it.

Feeding the 5,000

If you've opted for a hotel or restaurant reception, the food and drink really won't be a problem. Cost is another matter. Average wedding costs show that more is spent on the reception's food and drink than anything else. However there are ways to economize. Ask to see a variety of menus and try to negotiate a deal on the drink. In the end, you'll get what you pay for so hold out for the best options within your budget.

For those who set their hearts on some-thing a little more intimate at home, the word 'food' will take on a whole new meaning (think 'nightmare'). Catering your-self might seem like a good idea at the time, but the reality of getting your hat at the right angle while checking that the vol-au-vents aren't burning and that there are enough plates may prove too much for even for the most diligent among you. Even Margaret Thatcher didn't offer her pasta bake for Mark's wedding.

If you still remain undaunted, you'll need to plan the proceedings like a military campaign. Do not refuse offers of help, just make sure they are genuine and almost carved in tablets of stone. Some people may object to you faxing them daily to remind them about the coronation chicken, but you've got to be ruthless. She who hesitates ends up with an empty table and a houseful of ravenous guests desperately leafing through the phone book for a good Chinese take-away. Also, try and make sure your helpers stick to a dish they've cooked before; one that comes within their culinary range - better the bubble and squeak you know than the untried salmon en croute.

Honestly, organizing the Royal Tournament is less trouble. However if you're determined to press on, don't forget the hardware. There's nothing worse than a splendid spread all laid out and nothing to eat with.

You can't expect your guests to share the spoons, after all. For a sit-down affair you'll need the following:

- tables and chairs
- linen: table cloths and napkins
- dinner plates
- side plates
- cups and saucers
- serving plates and bowls
- cutlery, including cake forks
- tea spoons
- glasses
- dishes
- ashtrays
- bottle openers
- cake stand and knife

If you're not having a sit-down meal or enough food to approximate it, then the only precaution we suggest is to tell your guests. The natives do get a little restless if they've starved themselves for weeks in anticipation only to be offered garnished Ritz crackers. We've known of people hijacking trays of canapés after a foodless few hours and practically coming to blows over the last devilled prune.

Don't keep people waiting too long either. Unlike you they haven't passed the day in a state of nervous excitement, hardly able to manage any food. Chances are they'll be ravenous, and a bit of blotting paper with the first glass of champagne doesn't go a miss.

To make life a little easire and ensure that your mother manages to venture out of the kitchen to reveal her carefully chosen outfit from behind an apron, hiring waiters and waitresses is a great idea. This shouldn't cost too much. There are plenty of agencies who can advise on how many you'll need and whether they'll also help with setting up and clearing away afterwards. The mere fact that they're keeping everyone's glasses and plates filled, including yours, leaves you free to enjoy the party too. Remember, a small bribe given beforehand (known in the trade as a tip) should ensure smiling faces all round.

Even less trouble is leaving the worry

Silver horseshoes often decorate a wedding cake.
The silver respresents luck and the horseshoes symbolize protection.

about numbers of drumsticks and sausages to that happy breed - the professional caterer. These are people trained from birth to know how many stuffed mushrooms a grown man will consume in an evening. Even more impressively, which stuffing to use. This type of service ranges from Mrs Whatsit with her oven going nineteen to the dozen, churning out quiches galore; to Ms Lucinda Prior-Snell with her diploma from a Swiss finishing school who'll come round with her partner Bunty and create clever little sauces and suggest impertinent wines.

Obviously, what you'll end up paying varies enormously depending on the number of courses and the style of the food. Most caterers charge by the head, so it's best to ring around and compare quotes. Apart from food, you'll need to check if they provide crockery, glassware, etc. If they don't make a comprehensive list of every item required and book it well in advance. The names of companies who do this sort of thing can be found in the Yellow Pages. So there aren't any surprises on the bill, find out how much it will cost should Auntie Edna do her plate spinning act and it all goes horribly wrong.

THE CAKE

You'll probably feel that no wedding is complete without a cake. Since Roman times cakes have represented good luck and fertility - hence all the fruit and nuts. Even the marzipan is symbolic.

Cake-making is quite a cottage industry and there are lots of keen bakers around only too happy to show off their icing skills. Look in the local paper and ask around before committing yourself. You should try and sample some of their wares - just to check that their talents match your aspirations. The average cost of a wedding cake is £160, but if there's a recipe in your family for a spectacular Christmas cake then accept all offers to provide one for your wedding and simply pay for the ingredients.

Your venue may offer to provide an enormous cake and try and persuade you that four tiers are better than one. However, unless money is no object, all you really need is enough to give everyone present a little nibble. It's nice to have enough to send away slices to those not present, or to save for a subsequent christening, but it's not obligatory. Too much cake and it may all end in tiers ... ho ho!

Toasting the Happy Couple

The question of drink is a personal one, but if you've got no idea what to provide, as a rough guide you need something fairly

A recipe for bride's cake, published at the turn of the century:

1lb of love
1/2 lb butter of youth
1/2 lb good looks
1 lb sweet temper
1/2 lb blunder of faults
1 lb self-forgetfulness

1 oz pounded wit
1 oz dry humour
2 tbsp sweet argument
1 pt rippling laughter
1 1/2 wineglasses of common sense

Mix the love, looks and sweet temper into a well-furnished house; beat the butter to a cream; mix these ingredients well together with the blunder of faults and self-forgetfulness. Stir the pounded wit and dry humour with the sweet argument, then add to the above. Gently pour in the rippling laughter and common-sense, and mix thoroughly. Bake well forever.

decent to start everyone off (when there won't be the added benefit of food) and for toasts. After that the standard can drop somewhat.

Supermarkets these days are enormously geared up to guiding the novice or selling you just the beer or wine you've been looking for. Alternatively, you may have a friendly offie, satisfied to let you taste and try till you're happy (can we come?). They'll also probably let you borrow glasses for little or no fee, just a deposit. Your venue's banqueting manager or your caterer might also be able to make suggestions (watch out for the more expensive ones!) and give guidance.

In our experience you can *never* have too much drink (we didn't say 'too much to drink'!). But the average wedding budget dictates some kind of sensible plan when it comes to amounts. If money is no object, then shouts of 'drinks all round' will be greeted with hearty cheers. However most people need to work out how many glasses per bottle and per head and adjust the budget accordingly. If in doubt, seek advice.

But whether you plan on footing the entire drinks bill or simply the initial drinks and the toasts, make sure there's enough to go round.

If at some point the booze is going to stop flowing freely and the cash bar takes over, fair enough - only let your guests know the plan. Incidentally, this is when you discover which of his relatives are generous and which are unable to find their wallets. Take note: this sort of information is invaluable when you're in the middle of one of those 'your mother/father/sister ... always/never' type of rows. (Yes, you will have them, but you'll be armed. You'll thank us.)

By the way, don't forget to include plenty of tea, coffee and soft drinks in the calculations. These can be almost as welcome as flowing rivers of Australian Chardonnay. Well, maybe not that welcome, but you get the drift.

Speeches

No wedding is complete without a few words. The difficulty arises over people's interpretation of a few. At their best, speeches can be a source of great amusement for the listeners and not too terrifying for the speaker; at worse they can be an unending stream of dull stories and embarrassing jokes. Remember Tom's speech in *Four Weddings and a Funeral?*

The bridegroom gets away pretty lightly. As long as he manages to stammer out that immortal phrase 'my wife and I', and to thank his in-laws, parents and any other adoring relatives, he'll be regarded as a verbal genius. The only other thing he has to remember to do is to toast the bridesmaids ... that is if he can find a grill big enough. (Sorry, but we love this pathetic joke.)

Then we come to the best man. This is where the trouble really starts. Officially, all he's supposed to do is thank the bridegroom on behalf of the bridesmaids, read out a few telegrams, and propose a toast to the parents of the still-happy couple. Unfortunately tradition now dictates that he also regales the audience with a few choice stories about the groom's sordid past. The longer he has known your new husband the worse these can be. It must be pointed out to him, in very strong terms that the groom does not wish to spend his first night of wedded bliss explaining why three kissograms turned up on the stag night, no matter how funny it seemed at the time. Explain to him that these stories can be retold at the lads' get-togethers. (At this point neither will realize how infrequent these will be.)

Even if you actually approve of the choice of best man - and somebody out there must

- even the most meek and mild, good sort can be transformed by a bad attack of nerves fuelled by a stiff measure of Dutch courage – usually enough to float a small ferry. Once he staggers unsteadily to his feet, completely transfixed by terror in front of his expectant audience, the temptation to ditch the carefully though-out speech in favour of the one about ex-girlfriends and drunken exploits can prove too much.

Inviting the Masses

Once you've decided on the date, the type of wedding, the venue for the reception, and the guest list, *then* you can think about organizing and sending out the invitations.

Despite your wranglings over the guest list, you might as well resign yourselves to the fact that not all your carefully considered guests will be able to come. Uncle Fred might be away on a business trip (thank heaven for small miracles) and your favourite primary school teacher might be on holiday in Wales. This may not prove to be a complete disaster. The smart couple will have worked out a secondary or 'B' list of potential guests. As the responses flood in, make a note of those who can't come and quickly send off an invitation to the next person on your 'B' list. Whilst we would

caution you not to send out too many more invitations than your budget can handle, it's worth remembering that there may be some fluctuation in the figures. As a rough guide, for every ten invitations, figure on only seven or eight acceptances. This ratio may actually widen during the peak holiday months.

A Word about the Wedding Presents

There is no point in getting married just to get loads of new things. The price is too high, and there's nothing worse than being with the wrong guy even if you have got a lovely dinner service and a pressure cooker. Having established that he *is* Mr Right, you must now turn your attention to the contents of your future home.

There are, as ever, several ways of approaching the question of the wedding list. It is very useful for your guests to have some idea of what you'd like, and of course a list is the ideal way of avoiding the old cliché of getting five toasters and no waste paper bin, or whatever. It also means that everyone can find something they can afford - unless of course you leave a list at Cartier or Chanel.

Some stores offer such a comprehensive service that all your guests need to do is phone them, mutter 'number 23 in green' and leave their credit card number. A green toaster, beautifully wrapped and with a loving message, will then be delivered to you. The item in question is then removed from the list, so that latecomers to the telephone find they can only choose between a set of tea towels (rejected by everyone as being too cheapskate) and a solid silver punch-bowl with an unspeakable price tag. (If you're wondering what that item was doing in there anyway - your mother said you'd need it.)

To avoid this perhaps rather soulless approach and to give freedom of expression to the more creative and imaginative guests (in other words, those with enough time on their hands to go from shop to shop to find the perfect soap dish), you can combine the precise list with a few items that give freedom of choice. However, don't blame us if the one member of your family to exercise this right is the one who has being giving you 'interesting' and 'creative' things of such hideosity over the years that you hesitate to give them to a jumble sale.

Opinions vary as to when to make the list available to your guests. If you've registered with a specific store, a discreet line to that effect, slipped in with the invitation, should do the trick. Others prefer to wait until guests have responded to the invitation and

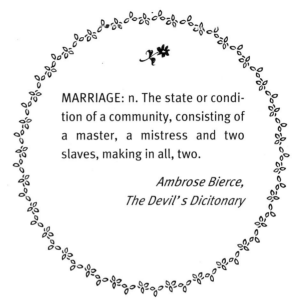

MARRIAGE: n. The state or condition of a community, consisting of a master, a mistress and two slaves, making in all, two.

Ambrose Bierce,
The Devil's Dicitonary

specifically asked for a list, or at least a few ideas. You'll no doubt save on postage and time if you choose the first option, but it doesn't really matter. Besides, there will always be those who use your list as a guide only - and then choose something completely different and utterly useless at the last moment.

One of our friends has solved the problem of 'I see you haven't got that nice crocheted loo roll holder, set of coasters with views of the Isle of Wight etc., etc. out then?' by keeping a list taped inside a cupboard full of such bits and pieces. At the first hint of a visit from Great-Aunt Clothilde she rushes to the cupboard and retrieves the nodding dog toothpick dispenser, putting it on prominent display.

This can backfire, though. Firstly, your friends may be rather startled by your sudden change in taste if they spot the thing without warning and take their cue when it next comes to buying you a present. Secondly, one of our friend's relatives, who thought they'd help out with a bit of housework, opened a cupboard to find the Mr Sheen and was confronted with a list beginning 'Uncle Fred: ghastly blue bowl, too small to be useful and too large to hide'. Relations - in both senses of the word - have been rather strained since.

DRESSED FOR THE PART

This should be one of the few occasions in your life when you will not be found sobbing into the duvet, surrounded by your entire wardrobe, shrieking, 'What will I wear?' And yet this very subject is likely to occupy 90 per cent of your waking hours during the build up. Let's face it, in reality you've probably been thinking about it since you were five.

Before that magic moment, when you enter the bridal department and actually qualify as being vaguely serious about buying something, try this simple exercise: find a mirror, stand in front of it and have a long, hard look at what is staring back. It may not be Kim Bassinger; it may even make Bernard Manning look reasonable; but this is what you are dealing with.

It is likely that the excitement and nervous exhaustion of the next few months will deal with a few extra pounds. If you feel you want to help the process along a bit, a diet is worthwhile embarking on (again). But be realistic - you're not about to be transformed from a statuesque 16 to a petite 8. Plastering photos of Christie Brinkley over your fridge door, far from dissuading you from eating, will only drive you to further gorging on chocolate cake. Remember, he proposed to you - cellulite and all, and may even have grown strangely attached to it over the time.

Don't feel a complete failure, or that your life and certainly your wedding day is ruined if you haven't reached seven stone. However, your day will undoubtedly be ruined if you *have* bought a dress several sizes too small, hoping to shrink into it.

Anyway, have you ever seen an ugly bride? Everybody looks good on the day. Call us slushy old romantics if you like, but it must be love.

Is That a Dress or a Meringue?

A glance through any wedding magazine (publications you will become chemically dependent upon), reveals a staggering range of dresses. Whichever area of your body you wish to conceal, there will be a frock to oblige. There are literally thousands of designs to choose from.

Once you've narrowed down the possibilities (if you can!), the only thing to do is to start trying them on. This can be a lot of fun for all concerned, particularly when you're being fussed over in some expensive designer's studio. But don't expect to come to a final decision in a hurry - these things take time. If you thought choosing a frock for the company's dinner-dance was a bit of a problem, multiply the anxiety level by 1,000 and you're approaching something close to the mark ....

It is surprising how many girls still go for virginal white and traditionally shaped dresses. Whatever your personal views of these creations beforehand, don't be shocked by your total conversion once you catch sight of yourself rising above the sea of froth and slipper satin. They are incredibly flattering, hide a multitude of sins and chocolate HobNobs, and are probably the only chance you'll get to look like a princess for a day.

This might seem like an over-the-top piece of advice, and indeed Caron laughed it off when someone said 'Don't forget to measure the width of the church aisle before choosing your dress.' But if you'd planned to have you and your father walking together up the aisle, and you and your husband side by side coming down it, it is good advice indeed. As it was, the unfortunate Mr Keating was forced to fight his way through yards of silk and lace and retain a respectful distance, even at the altar. Mind you, it could have been worse: the world's longest wedding dress train measured just over 97 feet 7 inches! The bridesmaids must have dropped exhausted by the wayside ....

These days really anything goes - long, short, rubber, tweed, and in a variety of colours from palest baby pink to bottle green check. If you're the slightest bit superstitious - and it takes a brave woman not to be by this stage - take note: it would seem that blue and white are the luckiest colours to choose.

Married in white,
> you have chosen aright

Married in blue,
> your lover is true

Married in pink,
> your fortunes will sink

Married in green,
> you will not long be seen

Married in red,
> you'll wish you were dead

Married in yellow,
> ashamed of the fellow

Married in brown,
> you'll live out of town

Married in grey,
> you'll live far away

Married in black,
> you'll wish you were back

In the end the best choice is the one that you feel most comfortable with. You might opt for the traditional meringue or skip the dress altogether and settle on the lime green leggings and the gold lamé top - just make sure you feel like a million pounds in your choice and you can't go far wrong. And don't feel too hide-bound by convention and tradition. After all, the Victorians often married in their 'Sunday best' (which could mean was a rather austere black number) and there have been countless registry office weddings in which the bride has shown a stunning display of creativity.

When it comes to cost, although the average price of a wedding dress is £525 - it can of course go very high. Go to Versace or Chanel and your one-off gown may cost £50,000. But don't faint - there *are* other options. There are plenty of places who will hire out dresses or that offer second-hand ones at reasonable prices. If your heart is set on something really romantic, why not

There are many superstitions associate specifically with the wedding dress. Possibly the most well-known is that it is unlucky for the bride to try on the dress and veil in their entirety before the wedding day. Also, the groom should not see the bride in the dress before the ceremony.

Important Accessories

Traditionally the bride wears 'something old, something new, something borrowed, something blue and a sixpence in her shoe'.

Something new: looks to the future and must be something either newly made or never worn before, e.g. the bride's dress or underwear.

Something borrowed: this is usually from a member of the family and refers to a link with the present. The idea is to borrow something small and perhaps precious, e.g. a prayer book, a veil, a piece of jewellery or a hair decoration. The tradition is said to be only valid if the object is returned after the wedding.

Something blue: blue is the colour of fidelity. The blue referred to for a wedding can either be worn to be seen, e.g. a blue trim on the dress or a flower in the bouquet; or can be worn hidden, e.g. in a garter.

Sixpence in her shoe: wishes the bride future wealth.

consider an antique dress? Some markets specialize in antique lace dresses (or indeed just the lace) and it may be just your luck to pick up a bargain and something really unusual (and that's *before* you find the dress). Plenty of girls also rely on their mums'/aunties' dress making skills and end up with the dress of their dreams for a fraction of the cost of those in the shops. However, be warned: this approach can significantly add to the stess level and is not to be recommended to those in 'difficult' mother-daughter relationships (who *isn't* in one of those at this stage?). Finally, you could bow to tradition and wear your mother's own wedding dress, if it's on offer. Just make sure it fits you *and* that you love it - it takes a brave woman to deny that!

The Bridesmaids and Attendants

Once you've got your own attire sorted out, it's time to turn your attention to the bridesmaids and attendants.

It may seem extremely tempting to dress them all in purple crimplene frills, to enhance your own gorgeousness on the day. The problem with this approach is that it won't encourage the fondest of thoughts from your assembled guests - think of the pictures - and if you're having page boys, it could leave them scarred for life. You're bound to regret it eventually, too. Relax - you *will* be the centre of attention on the day.

The original purpose of bridesmaids was to fend off evil sprirts, which is why they dress similarly to the bride - to confuse the spirits. But do remember, they come in different sizes: what looks cute on a three-year old can be frightening on a woman of thirty. They'll undoubtedly have their own opinions on what looks best but ultimately a compromise needs to be reached. In the end they are there to be your attendants and as such should not out-shine the bride.

While small girls are only too delighted to dress up for such occasions, page boys are a completely different kettle of fish. They will be horrified at your attempts to kit them out in velvet knickerbockers and buckled shoes, never mind the neatly combed hair. A hefty bribe at this point is very useful. It's easier than you'd imagine to conceal a Spiderman outfit under a 'Little Lord Fauntleroy' exterior - just make sure he's clear which way round they go.

Focusing on the Groom

Having got yourself and your various attendants sorted out, the spotlight falls on HIM. This really shouldn't be your problem, but invariably it is.

If you're really lucky he'll adopt the Beau Brummell approach and be so concerned about how it all looks that he'll be sneaking off to meet your dressmaker to make sure that your outfit comes up to scratch. Unfortunately this is an almost extinct breed. It's safer to assume that the vast majority of men are on the same wavelength as the page boy, and their idea of smartness is having their West Ham strip washed.

As far as the actual clothes go, his choice is almost as wide as yours. The traditional morning suit is still popular and is a good choice for the more conservative groom who is quite happy to let you hog the limelight. The more flamboyant can let rip with anything from brocade waistcoats and two tone shoes, to full Edwardian dress or fifties rocker gear. With any luck you'll be fully aware of these tendencies long before you catch sight of him on your way up the aisle.

Those hailing from a long way north of Watford may be entitled to wear full Highland regalia. It is quite staggering the number of males who having never shown the slightest interest in their cultural roots, suddenly acquire a keen taste for their knees and no underwear.

Ushers and the best man usually take their lead from the groom and in cases of reluctance can be told what to wear. So if you've ended up with an Elvis wannabee, the wedding party may look like a Showaddywaddy revival. The message here is *be firm*. This is *your* wedding and you don't want to be upstaged on the day.

That Very Important Person: Mother

And speaking of upstaging ... all these minor details pale into insignificance when it comes to the real person of the moment - your mother.

We strongly suggest that, like the Masons, there is an order of women whose members receive careful instruction on how the mother of the bride should look. This vivid mental picture may not match either her purse or, more worryingly, her figure. Weddings can have a curious effect on even the sanest of women. Don't let your mother's usual good taste and elegance fool you: she's just as capable of turning up doing a mean impression of Barbara Cartland as anyone else.

A combination of nerves and not wanting to overshadow the bride, but certainly to outdo the groom's mother, is to blame. Your tact and diplomacy, which may already be stretched, are needed once again to steer her through the minefield of unsuitable outfits and shop assistants on commission.

Sadly, you can have little infuence over what his mother wears, but try to stifle your screams or laughter. If by some strange twist of fate both mothers have gone for identical or at least similar outfits, usually it's the groom's mother who concedes and exchanges for another.

Trousseaus

Trousseaus always sound very exotic, but in fact consist of anything from sheets to bedsocks. These days it's more likely to be some new knickers from M & S. But it's still a good excuse for spending some more money on a 'going-away outfit'.

If you really are going away - straight on

to a fourteen-hour flight - a hobble skirt and 7" stillettos won't add to your in-flight comfort. While you may not want to bid farewell to your guests in an old tracksuit and trainers, don't forget to pack them in your hand luggage.

A New You?

There are two schools of thought on this subject: either you look more or less like you do normally, only tidied up a bit; or you choose a picture from a glossy magazine and decide that's who you'll be on the day. If you've chosen Cindy Crawford, do remember to leave enough time for the plastic surgery.

YOUR HAIR

Very few people will have the luxury of having a hairdresser constantly in attendance, unless of course like Lulu you had the foresight to marry one. Even then, they still might be too concerned with their own coiffeur to worry about yours.

If you're planning to radically change your look, a bit of practice beforehand may come in useful. It will add nothing to your day to discover, when the lacquer sets, that a beehive is for other birds. A few hours spent weeping in the lurid glare of the hairdressers are worth a lifetime of cutting yourself out of the wedding photos.

What we're trying to say here is understand your hair. If for the last few years it's been conducting an entirely separate life from your own, then make sure it knows your intentions. Introduce it early on to the joys of mousse, gel and the firm hand of a hairdresser.

As far as the finished style goes, something not too dissimilar to your own is probably best. There is a place for Bonnie Langford curls ... answers on a postcard please. Anyway, what's the sense in frightening the guy? If, however, you remain convinced that the hanging gardens of Babylon are just the thing for you, go ahead - we'd love to see the pictures.

Finally, remember to consider the veil and/or head-dress, if you've opted for them. There's no point in having a beautifully sculpted style if it's thrown out of whack by your crown of cabbage roses.

Don't forget to book an appointment with your hairdresser the morning of the wedding early on the proceedings. Impossible as it might seem, yours may not be the only wedding happening that day.

Your make-up

Wedding nerves affect people in different ways. If you know that you'll be given away by a red rash round your neck or alternately the pallor of Morticia, don't panic: where Mother Nature has failed you, the cosmetic counter will come to your rescue. Strange as it may sound, a particularly unfortunate shade of green stuff, worn under your normal foundation, makes you look less like someone in the last throes of scarlet fever and more like an English rose.

This is the sort of day when most of us feel that the natural look could do with a bit of a leg-up. If you're a bit doubtful about the inner workings of the make-up bag, it's well worth investing in an unbiased lesson. Go to any large department store and most make-up counters will have someone on hand to explain the mysteries of bronzing balls and free radicals. Be wary of those trying to entice you to buy all of this season's latest range - orange and turquoise may be in, but the pictures will tell their own sad story if they're not right for you. Try to avoid the type of assistant likely to send you out with bags full of stuff that you'll never use.

Whichever look you decide on - be it an evening out with Bet Lynch or as extra from The Sound of Music - practise beforehand and give yourself plenty of time on the day. If you really are all thumbs or just don't feel that you'll be confident enough on the day, enlist the help of a trusted friend to apply the goop and work her magic. Once again, practise with her beforehand so that there are no misunderstandings on the big day.

Finally ...

A word about leg-waxing, manicure and nail-extensions, colouring your hair or going on that amazing little diet that guarantees you perfect complexion ... plan ahead! These are not good ideas to have on the morning of your wedding. Nor is this the best time to try out a new perfume for the first time. Better stick to one that you love and that he can't resist!

DETAILS, DETAILS, DETAILS

By this stage you may be suffering from decision fatigue. You'll recognize the symptoms by the continual repetition of 'What do you think?' - 'I don't care!' Advanced cases will result in much door slamming and foot stamping, but don't give up yet - there's only a few more obstacles to go (a few hundred, that is). Before you get to the reception and get that champagne glass wedged firmly into your hand.

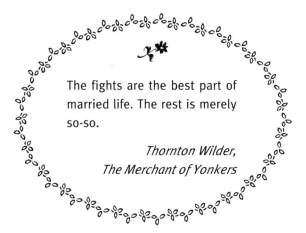

The fights are the best part of married life. The rest is merely so-so.

Thornton Wilder,
The Merchant of Yonkers

Say it with Flowers

Since mediaeval times flowers and weddings have been inseparable. And like just about everything else connected with weddings, there are endless superstitions and folklore about what your carry. For example, it is thought that extra luck will be bestowed on the bride who carries a sprig of white heather - the white symbolizing purity and light. The Victorians were great ones for finding

Bridal rose	*happy love*	Daffodil	*regard*
Garland of roses	*reward of virtue*	Dahlia	*instability*
Single rose	*simplicity*	Scarlet poppy	*extravagance*
Red rose bud	*pure and lovely*	Ivy	*friendship, fidelity*
White and red			*and marriage*
rose together	*unity*	Hollyhock	*fecundity*
White rose	*I am worthy of you*	White jasmine	*amiability*
Deep red rose	*bashful shame*	Yellow jasmine	*grace and elegance*
Dog rose	*pleasure and pain*	Sweet pea	*lasting pleasure*
Carnation	*alas for my poor heart*	Pinks	*woman's love*
Lily of the valley	*return to happiness*	Rosemary	*remembrance*
Honeysuckle	*bands of love*	Gladioli	*strength of character*
Lent lily		Ivy geranium	*bridal favour*
(wild daffodil)	*sweet disposition*	White lily	*purity and modesty*

meaning in the most unlikely symbols, thus the 'language of flowers' became very popular.

No matter what flowers you choose it's bound to mean doom and disaster, so you may as well pick what you like. But do bear in mind that the Venus Fly Trap indicates deceit.

If you're under five feet tall, you would be ill-advised to attempt to carry anything resemebling a hedge. A scaled down version will at least allow more than one of you down the aisle at a time and means that all that money spent on your dress wasn't wasted. Give the florist as much information as possible about the colour and style of yours and the bridesmaids' dresses. And if you're planning flowers for your hair, discuss the style and see if you can try out a sample before the big day. You don't want to find out you're allergic to freesias at the last minute.

These days you get what you pay for, and

the choice of flowers really is as vast as your budget can stand. Alternately, if you have a friend or someone in the family who can work miracles with a few roses and some trailling ivy, why not let them concoct something completely individual at a fraction of the cost of a professional florist? You can always get some suitable inspiration from all those bridal magazines you've been hooked on. Rip out a page and away they go!

Your florist will doubtless want to co-ordinate all the flowers, from the buttonholes to pew-ends. Just check with the vicar whether he/she minds his/her church being turned into the set of *Midsummer Night's Dream* or the Chelsea Flower show, with lilies on spikes being driven throught the pulpit. Caron's vicar did, and was found the night before the wedding hacking his way through the roses trying to find the altar.

As far as the reception goes, if yours or your father's pocket can stand it, go ahead and garland. It's worth bearing in mind, however, that by this stage most people's attention will have turned to drink, food and other people's hats. The florist is unlikely to share his view and will extol the virtues of flowers on every surface. Let them eat cake, or at least decorate it.

If the venue you've chosen looks a little bare - and let's face it, the scout hut can appear a bit gloomy on a November afternoon - there's no doubt that a few flowers do make a big difference. Something as simple as a few bunches of roses and a lot of trailing ivy cleverly arranged in swags can transform a place. For the more adventurous, arrangements involving dried flowers are one of those elastic items which can end up costing about five times more than you intended. So, wonderful as they look for a few hours, the day won't be ruined by the lack of a few

The bridal bouquet in olden times formed part of the wreaths and garlands worn by both the bride and groom. They were considered a symbol of happiness. In Wales bridesmaids are often given myrtle springs from the bride's bouquet to plant. Tradition has it that if one takes root, the young woman will marry soon.

bunches of chrysanthemums.

A cheaper decorative alternative is to use either crepe paper or coloured ribbons. Helium-filled balloons bobbing around, swags of muslin, or coloured netting decorated with cut-out stars or flowers will all help to create a party atmosphere. If you live near one of those shops selling fabrics for saris, you could invest in a few metres of some beautiful, shimmering fabric. Tulles, nylon nets and laces can look wonderful too, only make sure you don't get upstaged if you're similarly clad - this isn't the day for fading into the background. Think window dressing. You're not aiming for permanent or perfect, but effective and eye-catching. And don't forget to ask for help - you can't do everything on your own.

Transport

Unless you're the vicar's daughter, or a close neighbour, you'll need some sort of transport to carry you and your frock to the church. There's plenty of choice: you could have anything from a state landau with a pair of matched greys and a liveried groom, to a white vintage Bentley, or even a borrowed pie van.

If there's more than you and your dad to consider, you can do deals on a fleet of cars from a local taxi firm. Or cajole your friends into ferrying people about on the day. Just make sure they've managed to get rid of their smelly rugby kit and all those oily rags on the back seat before they show up to ferry Aunt Hilda about town. And make sure you get those promises in writing beforehand, otherwise your parents mightn't be too chuffed to find themselves hitching outside the church.

Registry office weddings don't always lend themselves to a big production number, with the only decoration on the cars parked outside likely to be a clamp. You'll probably just want to meet your guests and family there with maybe one flash getaway car for yourselves.

If you feel that you'll have enough to contend with on the day without half the town turning out to gawp at you, choose something discreet to arrive in. For the rest of us the sky's the limit - literally in the case of people who feel the need to parachute into their weddings. Others opt for hot air balloons, open-topped buses, cadillac and saxaphone, sedan chair, piggy back or motor bike (very popular with stylists and Hells Angels). And there are plenty of keen cyclists out there who've left for the reception on 'a bicycle built for two'. Just remember to keep your dress well away from the chain.

It's also just as well to remember that while the sun may be shining in your heart, on the day it might well have gone AWOL. So if blizzard conditions prevail, you need to have some sort of backup - or at least a pac-a-mac and a golfing brolly stashed away.

Finally, you'll need to book your transport early if you're planning anything a little bit special to remotely popular. It's surprising the number of people who opt for a horse and carriage in the middle of July. Aim to make a firm booking no later than six months before the event to avoid disappointment.

Recording the Magic Moments

You'll find that the day passes in such a blur of cake, champagne and tear-stained satin that you'll need photographic evidence to prove it actually happened and that you were there.

There are several options: you can rely on well-meaning friends with their Instamatics. This, however, is seldom without mishaps. Fogging film, events and people missed out entirely, and a Champagne Charlie approach may be just some of the delights awaiting you. On the plus side, this more informal approach often captures the atmosphere in a more relaxed way.

Another option is to bring in the professionals. While official photographers will ensure that every face and frill is logged for posterity, the worst of them can be a cross between a sergeant major and a Butlins Redcoat, forever forcing you into organized groups. Still, at least you can be guaranteed to have a decent (well, at least an undisputed) record of the big day.

Wedding photography is now such big business that many firms offer tantalizing incentives such as whizzing the photos back before the end of the reception so that Great-Aunt Zelma can get her order in, or even better, key rings with a photo of the happy couple as a sort of 'going home' present. Then there's the 'special-effect' photographs - plenty of soft focus and the dewy-eyed couple forever captured in a champagne glass surrounded by heart-shaped bubbles. Ask yourselves: do you really need or want these tacky gimmicks?

At the end of the day, professional photographers aren't cheap. In the overall wedding stakes, you'll only pay more for the reception and possibly the honeymoon. When it comes to deciding on the number and type of wedding shots, resist the photographer's more expensive suggestions. After all, does anyone actually *need* ten albums of wedding photos?

In spite of all that, you'll probably regret not having at least a few good pictures of the day - if only to prove later that you *can* look like a film star when you want to. The best idea is probably to have a set of organized official photos taken by a recommended professional, but to ask all your friends and relatives to send you their best efforts as well.

THE VIDEO

Now we get to the really good bit ... the video nastie. Beware the Jeremy Beadle approach, where canned laughter is added to your every grimace and stumble.

Even more worrying though is the keen amateur. He is likely to dog your every step - completely oblivious to the proceedings. When not enthusing about his state-of-the-art equipment, he will be concentrating on his fly-on-the-wall technique. Consequently, don't be surprised if the finished result consists of close-ups of you adjusting your knickers, Uncle Billy having that last-minte fag, and odd shots of your youngest bridesmaid picking her nose. The finer moments, such as the vows, or the best man's speech, are bound to be out of focus or lost behind a pillar, coupled with endless sound problems. This is a bleak picture, but there again so are most home videos.

The only answer is to find a professional. There are lots of companies who specialize in wedding videos. Thankfully they are also aware that they only get one opportunity and no rehearsals. As with all professional companies dealing with weddings, book their services early on. The summer months are a particularly busy time.

Initially your vicar may need gentle persuasion to allow you to film in the church. Once convinced though, the star-struck vicar is likely to turn your thirty-minute service into a two-hour audition.

Finally, don't forget to ask for the outtakes. You can never be too careful ...

Are We All Seated?

As the responses to your invitations flood in you should make a note of the acceptances and refusals. But the time will ultimately come when you are faced with another potential nightmare - the seating plan.

When you look at the names of all your friends and relatives you might despair of them ever surviving the meal without forks at dawn. Should you sit the withdrawn and silent ones beside the boozy jokers in the hope of igniting some small spark of friendship? Do you really want to subject a favourite aunt to the possibility of your flatmate's party trick with two oranges!

Perhaps it is best just to let them sort themselves out and sit wherever they want to, even if it means a scramble for the best tables and conspicuous gaps around unpopular members of the family. Only you can decide, because only you know what your guests are like. In theory, it would be lovely if everyone mixed together and got to know each other's friends and family; in practice, a bit of segregation isn't such a bad idea after all.

Most people can cope with meeting a few strangers, so long as they have some friendly faces for moral support when conversation dries up. So if you're having a big wedding with a wide variety of guests, a table plan gets them sitting down quickly and reassures them that they won't be stranded with only your two deaf aunts for company.

Put the plan where everyone can see it without having to fight their way through the hordes. As most people quite like to give up all responsibility of deciding who to sit next to, try to work out some sort of boy/girl arrangement. You can always use place cards to leave them in no doubt. At a smaller gathering it's more likely that your guests will sort themselves out without bloodshed. And if you've known each other for years, his relatives may be more familiar than some of yours.

Where you put all the children is also something to bear in mind. It's unlikely that they're going to stay the course from starter to speeches, so if you've got space, it's a good idea to put them all together within sight and sound of their supposed elders and betters. Usually they'll play together perfectly happily, and with any luck someone will appoint themselves honorary 'aunt' or 'uncle' and prevent the whole thing from ending in tears, leaving the parents to get quietly drunk. If you can't spare the room to create a special ghetto, then put the smalls where they can slide quietly off their chairs and go and play together (at least that's the theory).

With all the effort of getting your guests settled, you'll probably be too exhausted to pay much attention to where you and your gang should perch. You'll be glad to hear that tradition has taken care of all this for you in a way that ensures you're still the centre of attention, whether you want it or not. You'll finally get to speak to your newly acquired husband, not to mention taking the weight off your sling-backs.

At a seated meal, the main bridal party usually sits at top table, facing the guests. The bride and groom sit in the centre, with the bride on the groom's left and the bride's parents on either side of them:

Best man
Groom's mother
Bride's father
Bride
Groom
Bride's mother
Groom's father
Chief bridesmaid

If relationships between the two families are not all they might be, in the interests of a peaceful day, it might be better to seat them as follows:

Best man
Groom's father
Groom's mother
Bride
Groom
Bride's mother
Bride's father
Chief bridesmaid

If the parents of either bride or groom are divorced and remarried, their partners normally join the top table at either end:

Bride's stepmother
Best man
Bride's father
Bride
Groom
Bride's mother
Groom's father
Chief bridesmaid
Groom's stepfather

Thank-You Gifts

When all is said and done, organizing a wedding can faze even the calmest person. It's when you're faced with yet one more decision ('Is it to be green or pink crepe paper decorations?') that you value a second opinion from your chief bridesmaid. And even though you may want to ignore - better yet, gag - your mother more often than not, she still has been very helpful and a source of reassurance throughout the months (or so you keep telling yourself ...).

At this stage try to switch your focus on to them. Traditionally the bride and groom show their appreciation to their attendants with a token gift. It doesn't have to be huge, but in this case, the thought really does count. It might be a bottle of his favourite tipple for the best man (which may be more than he deserves, in your opinion) or a nice piece of jewellery or a prayer book for the bridesmaids. The message should be: thanks for putting up with all those dress-fittings and rehearsals, and for being there when needed.

As for your mother - and considering the costs, your father should really get a look in too - is there an adequate present? Probably not. Still, you can always take them out for a meal. Also, large but tasteful floral arrangements for your mother and a superb bottle for your dad will go some way towards saying thanks.

Consider buying the gifts before things get too frantic. A good time to present them might be just after the final rehearsal.

Leaving it all Behind: The Honeymoon

We know what you're thinking: this is a book about weddings, not beyond. Just how far are these women going to go? Don't worry we'll leave some of the future to modesty and chance. But before you get too caught up in all the arrangements you should spare a thought (or three) for booking your honeymoon.

It's important just to mention that some of the ground rules applied to the nuptials can be usefully applied a little further on. This is another time when well-meaning friends will be falling over themselves with piles of travel brochures to offer you advice. This will undoubtedly be based on their own experiences, either good or bad. Do feel free to ignore it all - you want to have your own honeymoon, not relive others.

People's idea of a good honeymoon does vary enormously. David Bellamy spent what he describes as a fascinating fortnight in a peatbog in Ireland. Lucky old Mrs Bellamy! But it wouldn't suit everyone.

The most popular destinations are:

1. Great Britain
2. The Caribbean
3. The USA
4. The Mediterranean
5. Africa and the Far East

As these places are popular you won't be the only ones flashing your new rings and ordering champagne, so make sure you book early. And remember to tell them you're on your honeymoon. Unless you're Jane Seymour, it'll be your only chance to make the most of it.

If you are heading off to somewhere foreign and exotic don't forget to have all the relevant injections. And stock up with insect repellent and diarrhoea pills - call us old

Marriage is popular because it combines the maximum of temptation with the maximum of opportunity.

G.B. Shaw

romantics - but an itchy fortnight spent studying the bathroom tiles is not the most auspicious start to any marriage. Of course it may bring you closer together, but it seems an almighty risk.

If you have excitedly booked your tickets in your new married name, make sure your old unmarried passport matches otherwise you'll need to bring a copy of your wedding certificate as proof of your new status. A few crumpled petals of confetti and a 'Just Married' sticker have little effect on passport control.

LAST-MINUTE FUN AND PANICS

The Irresponsible Bit: The Hen Night

Rather like a cheque this is one of those times when you should allow a decent interval for clearance .... Allow at least a week to get rid of:

- hangovers
- last-minute contenders for the part of potential husband
- serious doubts
- broken-hearted exes
- physical evidence of too good a time, eg. the tattoos, black eyes, love bites on the neck - basically anything that's likely to cause an awkward moment on the big day.

Although we're not suggesting that you should begin to take complete control of your fiancé's life, tell him he's well-advised to follow suit.

There's nothing more likely to end in tears than a group of friends, hell-bent on having a good time whilst under the influence of unlimited booze. It's really easy to get carried away. Whilst that all-encompassing phrase 'tired and emotional' will ring true; 'drunk, tired and emotional, while tied to a tree and handcuffed to a complete stranger' doesn't sound so good. Don't allow other people to egg you on. Often what seems like a bit of harmless fun at the time tends to get out of control and gossiped about in a way you hadn't intended. Aim to look back and giggle, rather than howl with embarrassment.

Ten Things Every Bride-To-Be Ought to Know

1. No matter how stringent your diet, you are unlikely to have lost quite enough weight to fit the dress - three sizes too small - you optimistically set your heart on.

2. All those ghastly relatives will be just as bad as you remembered them. Fortunately they will meet their match on his side.

3. Chomping your way through boxes of Rowntree's lime jelly, rarely ensures ten perfect nails. If by any chance you manage to achieve this miracle, you will undoubtedly have spots.

4. Despite all that practising of your marriage vows in what you fondly imagined was a loving way, on the day your voice will take on all the alluring qualities of Minnie Mouse on acid.

5. The green make-up which successfully changed your ruddy complexion to that of an English rose in the shop, will inevitably make you look green once you put it on at home.

6. Unless you are over six feet tall and weigh under five stone, an enormous bouquet could make it look as if you've inadvertently got hitched up to a roadside flower stall.

7. The name of your groom.

8. Have a good breakfast, because for the remainder of the day everyone will assume that the food of love is enough. It's unseemly to snatch at passing chicken legs.

9. You will recognize your husband-to-be, not because of the unearthly radiance softly playing about him, but because he's still got grease from his moped under his nails and a spot on his chin (ready to squeeze).

10. When your train needs retrieving from under the tenth pair of patent lace-ups, reluctant bridesmaids are nowhere to be seen, no matter how many Sindy bathrooms they've been promised.

Don't get us wrong - of course we want you to have a good time. We'll even pop in if you want. But try not to think of it as a goodbye to the single life and all that. Mind you, having spent a raucous evening dancing round your handbag, shouting at your friends, and refusing the advances of the local wolves ... you might be relieved to get away.

The politically correct version is a joint bash, which offers a delightful opportunity to see your intended rather the worse for wear (it will hardly be the last time, and something you may as well get used to). If you manage to agree on the venue and guest list for this event, as well as the arrangements for your wedding, it's probably a good omen. In fact, the world will beat a path to your door.

We've tried both the joint and separate approaches, and as you can see remained sober and upright! Not.

Final Checks

While you're recovering from the hen night, try to summon up enough energy to make those last-minute checks on all the arrangements. You need to focus on the main things: the actual ceremony, the clothes, the reception (including food, wine, cake, music, etc.), your transport, the photographer/video, and the honeymoon. Use the Wedding Day Planner at the back of this book to jog your memory and/or give yourself a fright.

Pre-Wedding Nerves

The night before your wedding - with your dress, hot-pants, leather skirt or whatever hanging outside the wardrobe; everything booked, cooked and ready - why do you feel that it would be quite nice if it all just stopped now? You suspect that if you left a note saying 'party on without us', some would prefer it - if they even noticed!

Some of us, not a million miles away from your humble authors, don't mind being centre stage; others loathe it - the thought of having to stand up in front of all those people is enough to bring on an attack of the vapours. Unfortunately, you're right to suspect that brides cannot avoid it. It might help to talk it over with someone who'll be sympathetic to your plight. This probably won't be your intended, who's more than likely feeling the same. The most important thing to remember is that you're not about to face a hostile crowd. Those who've survived, us included, will tell you there's nothing quite like walking into a sea of friendly faces, who are all there to support you. These people are people who love you;

they're happy for you; they'll think you're gorgeous - enjoy it.

The night before your wedding, those around you are likely to have mixed emotions. Even if you've been in the relationship for years, your family and friends will view your being husband and wife in a different light. You may find your parents getting a bit emotional about losing their 'little' girl (even if you're turning thirty and running your own company). But with all the planning and preparation out of the way, you can spend time together relaxing - knowing it's too late to do any more organizing.

In fact, unless you're greeting hordes of visiting relatives, the best thing to do is have a few (and we mean *just a few*) calming drinks - anything from neat gin to Horlicks, watch a soothing film (not *Fatal Attraction*) and think beautiful thoughts. There's no point having an early night because you won't sleep properly. But this isn't the night for a final fling at the local disco either, although it's fun to have a few good friends round for a last girly sleep-over.

Pre-wedding nerves are fine. The only time to worry is if you have to be dragged screaming from the house.

The Big Day is HERE!

6 a.m. - 'OH NO, IT'S RAINING!!'

Undoubtedly you'll waken at some unearthly hour, realize that this is it, and then rush to the window to see what the weather's up to. We know it seems impossible that it could rain on the day, but remember - the wedding can still take place. The guests and you will enjoy it anyway, even if you are a little damp.

GETTING READY

Now the trick is to get yourself ready without panicking. Readers of *Jackie* magazine (sadly

---

✍♥~ ✍♥~ ✍♥~ ✍♥~ ✍♥~ ✍♥~ ✍♥~ ✍♥~ ✍♥~

If a bride wakes up to a chirping bird on her wedding day, this is said to bode well for her marriage. However the opposite is said of the bride who breaks anything on her wedding day.

✍♥~ ✍♥~ ✍♥~ ✍♥~ ✍♥~ ✍♥~ ✍♥~ ✍♥~ ✍♥~

A bride should never look at herself in the mirror when she is completely ready to leave for church. She should have a final check in the mirror, but leave just one thing still to put on, however small. Victorian brides achieved this by putting on their gloves at the last moment. This superstition stems from the old mirror belief that part of oneself goes into the reflection and that it would be a bad start to her married life if the bride gave less than her whole self to her new husband.

Also, couples should not see each other on the day until they meet at the altar. However, if they happen to look in a mirror together after the marriage, this is said to be a good sign.

no longer with us) will remember those ridiculous timetables which told you how long you should allow to get yourself ready for a party: 10 a.m. - paint your toe nails; 11 a.m. iron your dress; 11.30 - find a boyfriend; etc. Well this is probably the only day of your entire life that it actually applies.

If you have a houseful of guests - give yourself bathroom priority. People will want to wait on you hand and foot - let them. Enjoy breakfast in bed and perks like not touching anything during the full fifteen minutes while your nails dry. If you're having your hair done - book yourself an early appointment or arrange for someone to come to the house to give you a hand with that and your make-up. Give yourself plenty of time so that you can enjoy every minute of being pampered throughout the day, rather than rushing about and working yourself into a sweat.

If at this stage you realize that you've forgotten something - guests, flowers, a band - do what you can but don't worry. If things don't go according to plan - change the plan. As long as you've got each other and the presiding official, you're okay. Short of facing fire and pestilence, the odd setback won't matter - look on it as anecdotal material for your children.

As far as the eating goes, head for the carbohydrates - the dress will still fit and you'll need the energy to get you through the day. Unless you're aiming for an appearance on *You've Been Framed*, we don't advise fainting at the altar.

When you're all bathed, crimpled and resplendent in your wedding finery, we've found a small thimble full (well actually a large glass) of champagne provided the necessary Dutch courage. This is traditionally when your father or someone close whispers 'you don't have to go through with this, if you don't want to' - though quite what their reaction would be if you asked them to help you escape is difficult to say, but it's nice of them to offer.

As you gaze admiringly at yourself for a final check, you'll realize there's something missing - HIM. Traditionally couples spend their last unmarried night apart, so you'll find yourself actually looking forward to seeing him again. When you do meet up, we guarantee that the expression in his eyes will prove to you that you're doing the right thing. All the endless planning, agonizing, choosing, dieting, and the overdraft will have been worth it. We would never have written this book if we didn't think weddings were Good News. There's nothing like a happy ending.

GET ME TO THE CHURCH (OR WHATEVER)

All that remains is to have a wonderful day - one that will get your marriage off to the best possible start. No amount of organizing or even money will help you with the next bit ... it's down to you two.

Once you arrive at the church (or whatever) it's 'all systems go'. Still, things *have* been known to go wrong at this stage. But don't panic - there's no use in worrying about it now.

Whether you and your groom decide on the old or the new service, don't worry about making mistakes. Your minister will guide you through, as nerves can play havoc with your words. Charles and Di spring to mind: they got their words muddled - mind you, they seem to have got lots of things muddled !

Throughout this book we've been referring to traditional wedding legends and superstitions. Most of them are connected

The old tale that it was lucky for the couple to encounter a chimney sweep on the way to church goes back to the days when people believed that soot and ashes were symbols of fertility.

79

with the bride or weddings in general. The bridegroom does not have many superstitions attached to him, however there are a few. He must not drop his hat or, more significantly, the ring. Should the bride have to help him put the ring on her finger during the ceremony, he can expect her to be the boss in the future. Finally, on no account must he go back for anything after the wedding journey has begun.

Savour every moment of this part of the day - you'll never be able to repeat it just as it happened. If you're like most people, the words 'blissful happiness' will seem like a huge understatement and the ceremony, in hindsight, will have rushed by in an amazing blur.

POP THOSE CORKS!

Now that it's all legal you can really relax and have a good time. Well, nearly. There is the obstacle of the receiving line, which is the age-old practice of remembering exactly who you've invited to the shindig and being kissed by all of them, so that you and your husband end up with a vermillion cocktail of assorted lipstick smudges on both cheeks and the bewildering feeling that perhaps you're at the wrong wedding.

As it may be the only opportunity to have at least a quick chat with everybody, it is worth doing, as long as you bear a couple of things in mind. There is an art to making people feel welcome without giving them half an hour each. For practise in this area, watch some sort of chat show, or study royal walkabouts in detail. Also, remember there are people waiting further down the line who are probably just as desperate to sit down as you are, if not more so. If they're queuing in a draughty corridor, the excitement of the impending festivities will have lost much of its appeal.

What happens at your reception is entirely up to you and your guests. But there are a few traditional 'entertainments' which your guests in particular might look forward to. No, we don't mean the speeches ... we mean, of course, the throwing of the bouquet, and the garter ritual.

The other custom of throwing the garter began in France, where pieces of bridal attire were considered lucky. The bride would throw the garter to the guests at the wedding feast and whoever caught it would be supposedly blessed with good luck. In the United States the groom removes the bride's garter and throws it to the unmarried men. The man who catches it is thought to be the one who will marry next. He then replaces the garter on the leg of the woman who catches the bridal bouquet.

Today the practice of tossing a bouquet is

Let them eat cake ...

There are numerous legends and customs surrounding the wedding cake:

• The wedding cake has symbolized fertility since Roman times.

• The custom of the bride cutting the first slice was supposed to ensure a fruitful marriage. But in Britain and Europe a couple ensures good luck and happiness by cutting the first slice together, to show they intend to live in harmony and share everything.

• In parts of the world the eating of cake by a man and a woman actually constituted a wedding.

• For centuries in England it was the custom to throw slices of the wedding cake over the bride's head to ensure she bore children.

• No bride should ever make her own wedding cake or taste it before the appropriate time.

• There is an old saying that the bride who keeps by her a piece of wedding cake also retains the love of her husband.

• It was the Chinese who began the custom of giving all friends present at a marriage ceremony a slice of cake, and of sending pieces to those not able to be present, so that all may enjoy good luck.

a refined development of throwing the garter. The bouquet is meant to be tossed at random, but you'll probably find that your unmarried friends have perfected catching skills to rival Ian Botham's. Again, the lucky lady who catches the bouquet is believed to be the next to marry.

One of the ironies of the wedding party is that you spend months meticulously plan-ning the best party ever and then leave just when it's getting good. Of course you don't have to go, but if you've got a plane to catch there's no choice. Traditionally the send-off of the bride and groom is an important part of the event. There is a certain breed of guest who feels deprived if they haven't seen you struggle to drive away hampered by a lip-stick-smeared windscreen and a ton of hardware dangling from your bumper. They know who they are ...

Actually, the custom is to decorate the car and tie an old shoe to it. The origin of this custom is a little obscure, but it could date back to Anglo-Saxon times when it was customary for the bride's father to give one of his daughter's shoes to the groom. He would then touch his new wife with the tip of the sole to indicate who was master and that the authority over the woman had now passed from father to groom. In Greek ceremonies today, the dominating partner is decided by whoever is the first to tread on the other's foot - the bride or groom - at a designated stage of the ceremony.

Take it from me, marriage isn't a word ... it's a sentence.

King Vidor

THE AISLE HIGH CLUB

The one very important part of your marriage where friends and family are definitely not welcome is beyond the bedroom door, when you finally gain membership to the Aisle High Club.

The theory is that this is the night of nights: every teenage magazine built up your hopes, and every old film to the sort of musical crescendo that signified that beyond the closed bedroom door all hell was breaking loose.

Get real.

You'll have been up most of the night before; your stomach will have been in knots all day; you'll have danced your stilettos to the sole and celebrated wildly. When you finally reach your bed, no matter how kingly the size and how silken the sheets, there's only one thing you'll want to do: sleep.

Rejoice in a quickie, knowing that you've got your honeymoon and the rest of your lives together. Don't feel disappointed ... you're not alone.

Just Before We Go

We know this will sound strange coming from two people who've just written an entire book on the subject, but remember - it

It was considered extremely unlucky for the bride to stumble on entering her house for the first time. This is one of the reasons why the groom carries the bride over the threshold. Another old Roman explanation is that she was not to touch the house until she was officially part of it by eating wedding cake at the hearth.

is only a wedding, a *start* to your life together rather than an end in itself. Some bits of it, of course, need to be taken more seriously than others, but overall we hope you find more to enjoy than panic about and that there aren't too many situations that you can't make the best of. Basically, as long as you both turn up and are still pleased to see each other, then you're on to a good thing. Remember, it's a large spot that can't be covered with concealer.

Relax, have fun, send us the photos, and ultimately an invite to the Silver Wedding party.

P.S. If it does all go horribly wrong long-term, we'd love to hear your stories for our follow-up book *Divorce: The Best Bits*

WEDDING DAY PLANNER

Twelve/Six Months

Decide where you want to get married and see the minister, priest or rabbi to book the date. Registry Office weddings can only be booked three months in advance.

Agree a budget with your family and fiancé so that you can keep a check on outgoings. Also, decide upon how many people will be invited and work out a guest list.

Book caterers, reception venue and entertainment. Summer weddings are very popular and generally need to be arranged several months in advance. Hotels and halls can usually only cater for one or possibly two weddings per day.

Contact several caterers and hotels in the area and compare the facilities offered by each. If possible, try to have a meal at the venue beforehand to get some idea of their standards. Some hotels accustomed to this type of catering offer a wedding package, which might include wedding cake and stand, toastmaster, flowers and a room in which to get changed. Naturally the cost of food and drink will depend on your own personal choices. Ask the caterers for sample menus and a list of drinks that they have available. Try to obtain at least three different estimates. Once you have found a caterer which fulfils all of your requirements within the budget you have set make a definite booking.

Book a professional photographer and video company. Organize your wedding cake if the hotel are not providing one.

Choose bridesmaids, best man and ushers and start looking around to see what you and the groom are going to wear. Book a designer well ahead if dress/shoes/bridesmaid's dresses are being made.

Organize all wedding flowers including bouquets, head-dresses, buttonholes, and those for the wedding ceremony and the reception.

Book cars, especially if you want something different and make firm arrangements with friends or family to help out with transport on the day.

Book your honeymoon now in order to avoid disappointment. Popular destinations and bridal suites are often fully booked in high season.

Consider taking out an insurance policy against possible disasters such as damage to your dress or photographs.

Four/Three months

Confirm arrangements with the person who is performing your ceremony. Discuss with them the service, music, bells and church fees. Also discuss flowers you are planning and whether confetti is allowed.

Book registry office ceremonies now.

Finalize your honeymoon plans. Arrange for visas or any vaccinations necessary for foreign travel. Bear in mind that if you want to change your passport to your married name, it takes at least six weeks.

Shop for your going-away outfit and honeymoon clothes.

Check that a hotel room has been booked for the night of your wedding.

Place an order for your wedding stationery, including invitations and envelopes, Order of Service sheets and wedding cake boxes. You may also like to order march books, printed napkins, menu cards, place cards and wedding favours.

Choose your wedding ring (or rings if you are both having one).

Two Months

Send your invitations out at least six weeks before the wedding and record acceptances and refusals as they come in.

Send out a gift list to those who request it. Send thank-you letters on receipt of gifts.

Ensure that your guests have maps to all venues and details of local accommodation.

Choose presents for your attendants, bridesmaids, best man, mothers etc.

One Month

Finalize numbers for the reception and inform the caterers in writing at least two weeks prior to the wedding day.

If not already done, buy cake boxes for guests unable to attend.

Check that all the wedding clothes for you, your groom and all attendants are near completion.

Visit your hairdresser with your head-dress, plan the style for your wedding and book your final appointment. If you are styling it yourself, have a practice run. This also applies if you are having a make-up artist for the day or intend to do it yourself.

Check that all transport arrangements are finalized and time the journey.

Order any traveller's cheques and currency for the honeymoon.

If you plan to change your name or address, notify your bank, building socity, doctor, friends, etc., etc.

Contact your local paper if you want them to cover your wedding or to book an announcement.

Arrange hen and stag nights, but don't make them the night before the wedding!

One Week

Make final checks on all details - cake, flowers, photographers, etc.

Make final checks on the honeymoon arrangements.

Have a rehearsal of the ceremony and check that service sheets have been delivered to the best man.

Make final checks on your clothing and wear in your wedding shoes at home.

Ensure that morning suits or any other hired items are collected.

The Wedding Day

Ask family and friends to see that the following arrangements are made for you:

- your honeymoon case is sent to the hotel
- after you've changed into your going-away clothes at the reception, your wedding dress and the groom's suit are packed and taken home
- wedding presents are packed and taken to your home
- hired items are returned
- wedding cake is sent to those unable to attend

WEDDING ANNIVERSARIES

First	*Paper*	Fourteenth	*Ivory*
Second	*Cotton*	Fifteenth	*Crystal*
Third	*Leather*	Twentieth	*China*
Fourth	*Books*	Twenty-fifth	*Silver*
Fifth	*Wood*	Thirtieth	*Pearl*
Sixth	*Iron*	Thirty-fifth	*Coral*
Seventh	*Wool*	Fortieth	*Ruby*
Eighth	*Bronze*	Forty-fifth	*Sapphire*
Ninth	*Pottery*	Fiftieth	*Gold*
Tenth	*Tin*	Fifty-fifth	*Emerald*
Eleventh	*Steel*	Sixtieth	*Diamond*
Twelfth	*Linen*	Seventieth	Platinum
Thirteenth	*Lace*		